Group interactive art t

As a result of her wide experience as an art psychotherapist and group therapist, Diane Waller believes strongly that the use of images within the dynamic framework of a group can greatly increase the potential curative and change-provoking elements at work. In her new book, she presents the first theoretical formulation of a model which integrates the change-enhancing factors of both group psychotherapy and art therapy, showing how the theoretical model works in practice through a series of illustrated case examples. By testing the model in clinical and educational situations, she demonstrates that it can be adapted for use with a variety of client groups, in short- and long-term contexts, and with trainees from different disciplines and from different societies and cultures.

Diane Waller's extensive practical experience of running training workshops with a wide variety of different groups, both in Britain and elsewhere, gives *Group Interactive Art Therapy* a valuable multi-cultural dimension. It will appeal to an international readership of art therapists, group therapists and others wishing to understand more about the theory and practice of this specialised form of art psychotherapy.

Diane Waller is Head of the Art Psychotherapy Unit, Goldsmiths' College, University of London.

Group interactive art therapy

Its use in training and treatment

Diane Waller

London and New York

First published in 1993
by Routledge
11 New Fetter Lane, London EC4P 4EE

Simultaneously published in the USA and Canada
by Routledge
29 West 35th Street, New York, NY 10001

Reprinted 1996

Routledge is an International Thompson Publishing Company

©1993 Diane Waller

Typeset in Times by Witwell Ltd, Southport
Printed and bound in Great Britain by
Biddles Ltd, Guildford and King's Lynn

A Tavistock/Routledge Publication

British Library Cataloguing in Publication Data
A catalogue record for this book is available from the
British Library.

Library of Congress Cataloguing in Publication Data
Waller, Diane, 1943-
    Group interactive art therapy: its use in training and
    treatment by Diane Waller.
    p.   cm.
    Includes bibliographical references and index.
    1. Art therapy. 2. Group psychotherapy. I. Title.
    [DNLM: 1 Art Therapy – methods. 2. Psychotherapy,
    Group – methods.
    WM 450.5AB W198g]
    RC489.A7W365 1993
    616.89'152 – dc20
    DNLM/DLC
    for Library of Congress   92-49164
                                                         CIP

ISBN 0-415-04843-5 (hbk)
ISBN 0-415-04844-3 (pbk)

Contents

Illustrations

PLATES

Section I

Introducing group interactive art therapy

Introduction

A BRIEF DEFINITION OF GROUP INTERACTIVE ART THERAPY

The model of 'group interactive art therapy' is based on concepts from group analysis, interactive (or interpersonal) group psychotherapy, systems theory and art therapy. It is an evolving model which in its theoretical base incorporates the work of Foulkes, Stack Sullivan and Yalom; and latterly Agazarian and Peters and Astrachan, who have attempted to introduce a 'systems approach' to group psychotherapy.

Group interactive art therapy draws on fundamental principles of art therapy. These are: that visual image- (or object-) making is an important aspect of the human learning process; that image-making (and this includes painting, drawing, clay-work, constructions, etc.) in the presence of a therapist may enable a client to get in touch with early, repressed feelings as well as with feelings related to the 'here-and-now'; that the ensuing art object may act as a container for powerful emotions that cannot be easily expressed; and that the object provides a means of communication between therapist and patient. It can also serve to illuminate the transference (that is, feelings from the past which are brought into the here-and-now and influence the way that we experience others) between the therapist and patient.

I have begun the exploration of this model by giving an idea about the way in which concepts of group psychotherapy and art therapy have evolved from about the 1940s. I have included discussion of the work of art therapists who have written about groups, particularly the group analytic or interactive models. I have drawn attention to the debate in art therapy literature about 'directive and non-directive' approaches to art therapy and their relative merits, which was launched by McNeilly in 1983, and shown how this gave rise to an interesting discussion about the role of theme-centred interaction in art therapy groups and about structuring the group's time between image-making and talking. Throughout the book I have drawn fairly extensively on those authors who have presented and developed the 'interpersonal' approach to group psychotherapy (for example, Yalom, Ratigan and Aveline, Bloch and Crouch).

Introducing art therapy to an interactive group changes the dynamics of the group. I have pointed out aspects of the interactive group which are generally held to be curative and described how art therapy may enhance the treatment potential of the group. At the same time, the introduction of art materials makes specific demands upon the conductor and the group members and I have explored what I feel are the main issues involved in the leadership of an interactive art therapy group.

The theoretical elements of the book are illustrated by examples from practice – my own and others – to show how the model can be adapted for use with trainees from different backgrounds (medicine to art) and clients (from more or less well-functioning adults to people with mental handicaps). As one of the most important learning experiences for me has been in working abroad in societies and cultures very different from that of the UK, and I firmly believe that therapists need to be aware of their own cultural and racial biases, I have tried to give the book a 'cross-cultural' flavour. I have tended to use 'client', 'patient', 'participant' and 'member' to describe group members, depending upon the context of the group.

Names of all participants and, in some cases, the location of the group have been changed in order to protect confidentiality.

I would like to acknowledge the following, with grateful thanks:

all the group members and interpreters,
Centro Italiano di Solidarieta, Rome,
Centre for Arts and Therapy, Athens,
Medical Academy, Sofia, Bulgaria,
Department of Psychiatry, University of Zagreb,
Teresa Boronska,
Dan Lumley,
Netherne Hospital, Coulsdon, Surrey (photograph of the studio),
Nick Tipton (photograph of the Art Psychotherapy Unit hut),
Juan Corelli,
Nizetta Anagnostopoulou,

without whose help the book could not have been written.

Chapter 1

Groups and art therapy

SOME BRIEF BACKGROUND NOTES ON GROUP PSYCHOTHERAPY AND ART THERAPY

The theory and practice of group psychotherapy, in its many forms, has been well documented; that of art therapy, less so. Events following the Second World War led to group psychotherapy and art therapy being integrated into rehabilitation movements – especially into the rehabilitation of war-traumatised victims. In 1942, Wilfred Bion from the Tavistock Clinic was placed in charge of the military training and rehabilitation wing of Northfield Hospital where he had to rehabilitate and return up to 200 men to the army. He used 'group dynamics' to encourage the men to learn a way of coping and adapting to inter-group tensions. Although Bion and his colleague Rickman were successful in rehabilitating many patients, their approach was not appreciated in the prevailing military-oriented system and they were transferred. Foulkes went to Northfield in 1943 where he joined Harold Bridger, Joshua Bierer and Tom Main. They too made use of group psychotherapy but took care to integrate their approach into the overall treatment philosophy and hence were able to stay on, with much success (see Main, 1946; Foulkes, 1948; Aveline and Dryden, 1988). After the war, Bion, Sutherland and Bridger went to the Tavistock Clinic and were joined by Henry Ezriel. Foulkes went to the Maudsley and Main went on to the Cassel Hospital where he developed the concept of an analytically-oriented therapeutic community. Joshua Bierer organised social clubs among patients, using Adlerian concepts as a basis for his work (see Bierer, 1948). He was responsible for forming the British Association for Social Psychiatry which emphasises the importance of patients' own contribution to their treatment programmes.

In 1952 the Group Analytic Society was formed, together with a journal, *Group Analysis*, and later the Institute for Group Analysis was established by Foulkes and played a central role in developing training and standards of practice.

In the USA, important advances, deriving from social psychology, were made by Kurt Lewin and his colleagues. Lewin proposed that an individual's personal dynamics are bound up with the social forces which surround him or her (Lewin, 1951). Just after the Second World War, Lewin used his model to train community leaders who were trying to work with multi-cultural groups where there was much racial tension. The National Training Laboratory was formed in 1950. The aim of the laboratory was to provide a training for participants from many different professional backgrounds in group work and interpersonal dynamics so that they might more effectively conduct their own groups. This was the beginning of the 'Sensitivity' movement, which led to the 'Encounter' movement and to the development of 'Esalen' in California in 1962. Numerous similar centres developed all over the USA and elsewhere, including in Britain (e.g. Quaesitor, in London). The Encounter movement was to have a strong influence on some British art therapists in the late 1960s and early 1970s.

Ruitenbeek (1970) points out that, regardless of claims made by various people as to their being the 'inventors' of group psychotherapy, it is clear that no one person was the originator and that in itself might have been a reason for group psychotherapy being conceived and developed in a fairly 'open' context. In contrast, even though the situation has obviously changed to some extent in the past two decades, not only because of the changing attitudes among 'orthodox' psychoanalysts but because of the changing sociological context in which treatment of so-called mental illness takes place, individual psychoanalysis was and is still tied to the heritage of Freud and many techniques and styles are part of his work and inventive spirit.

Ruitenbeek suggests, and I am inclined to agree with him, that in a dynamic and pragmatic society like the USA, orthodoxies do not last long, or they are questioned and new models arise as a result of the synthesis of old and new. Experimentation within the confines of traditional psychoanalysis is difficult but group psychotherapy provided the right kind of framework for such experimentation – for example, in time (not being tied to the 50 minute hour), in manner of approach (psychodrama, encounter, etc.).

Individual analysis, confined as it often is to the wealthier strata of society, has been less able to cope with problems engendered by the pressures of change and breakdown of secure networks in modern day life – not only in the West but world-wide – which leads people to feel alienated and unable to make close relationships. Many patients who are referred to, or refer themselves to, psychotherapists, have problems which turn out to be mainly societal in origin, and although there is usually also a personal component, it is not helpful to 'pathologise' the patient's problems. This is particularly important when considering the treatment of persons from different cultural or ethnic backgrounds to the prevailing one, and recent research (begun by Littlewood and Lipsedge, 1982) reveals the dangers inherent in failing to take this into account. One of the most telling conclusions of their current research is that mental illness can be an intelligible response to racism and disadvantage.

Clearly then, group psychotherapy could prove an important medium in which to explore, come to terms with and, more importantly, change an intolerable situation in one's life through intimate contact with others. It could also present an opportunity to enrich those relationships already existing, even if limited by physical disease or mental handicap. There is still a lack of awareness among general practitioners and other referring agencies about the value of group psychotherapy. This, combined with the reservations and anxieties that people may feel when a group is mentioned, means that many people who could benefit from groups are instead referred for individual psychotherapy or counselling. Worse, they might be referred to a group because it is 'cheaper', thus giving the impression that it is an inferior form of treatment, which it most emphatically is not. It is to be hoped that through increasing training in group psychotherapy for health care professionals, teachers, social workers and other workers engaged with the general public, such attitudes will change.

As far as the history of art therapy is concerned, it too depended partly on the Second World War rehabilitation movement for its development in Britain. There had been, however, a tradition of artists going to work in hospitals (both general and psychiatric) throughout the early part of the century. Often their aim was to provide a relaxing and creative release from the tedium of convalescence following a serious operation or during a long-term illness such as tuberculosis. Occasionally artists were asked by doctors to stimulate patients to produce paintings which could be used as an aid to psychiatric diagnosis.

The term 'art therapy' was first coined in 1942 by the artist Adrian Hill to describe the work he was doing with recuperating tuberculosis patients at the King Edward VII Sanatorium in Sussex. He discovered that not only did painting provide patients with a way of passing the time but it gave them a medium through which to express anxiety and trauma. Being an energetic, well-known public figure, Hill conducted successful campaigns to have 'art therapy' used more widely, in general and psychiatric hospitals as well as sanatoria.

It was also in 1942 when Rita Simon, an artist and illustrator, 'accidentally' began to work in Joshua Bierer's patients' social club in north London. Her developing interest in Adlerian psychology and later her own analyses, combined with her deep involvement in art, led to a long and distinguished career in art therapy.

In the 1940s and 1950s, it is fair to say that, within the hospital system, art therapy was not practised as a form of psychotherapy, but it provided a valuable expressive outlet for patients who could not respond to verbal therapy (e.g. long-stay, chronically ill, psychotic). It was however incorporated into a psychodynamic model of treatment in some private centres, notably the Withmead Centre, which was founded by Dr Irene Champernowne, a Jungian analyst, and her husband, in 1942. Other psychoanalysts also made extensive use of drawings as a central aspect of their work (Milner, 1950, 1969; Winnicott, 1951, 1971).

Art therapy developed two parallel strands: art as therapy and art psychotherapy, with Hill representing that aspect of art therapy which emphasized the 'healing' potential of visual art activity and Champernowne the importance of the relationship between the therapist, the patient and the art object – which included paying attention to transference phenomena. These two strands have, to some extent, merged over the years but there is still a lively debate in progress (focussed on the name of the profession: art therapy or art psychotherapy) as to the true essence of art therapy. There is no doubt (according to the literature at least) that art therapists today place more importance on the dynamics of the therapist–patient–object interaction, which in no way detracts from the power of the image to communicate, express and aid integration of conscious and unconscious processes.

Today, art therapy is a regulated profession with approximately 700 registered members. Training is at postgraduate level and all three approved programmes are in the state higher education system: at Goldsmiths' College, University of London; Hertfordshire College of Art and Design, St Albans; and the University of Sheffield. (See Waller, 1991 for a detailed account of the history of art therapy and the issues touched upon above.)

USING ART THERAPY IN GROUPS

In the following section I will outline some of the main developments in the use of art therapy in groups, mainly by reference to the literature in Britain and the USA.

The work of some of the pioneers of art therapy certainly involved group work, usually in open studio settings, with an informal structure rather like that found in art school studios of the time (1950s and earlier). When they worked in hospitals, the majority of art therapists were reliant on their own experience of studio groups, or of teaching in adult education classes or school. In the hospital groups, patients would come and go, paint and draw in their own time when the studio was open and the therapist present. The interaction between the tutor/therapist and the individuals in the room reproduced a familiar art student–tutor dynamic: individuals could discuss their work with the therapist and as this was supposed to be 'private' it often consisted of whispered conversations in a corner of the room to the exclusion of other patients. Patients were often subtly influenced by each other's productions in the shared space of the art room. The space became like the artwork itself – personal yet at the same time public and shared – and could be entered at the discretion of the artist/tutor-therapist.

Art therapy groups (as opposed to studio sessions) evolved in the late

1960s out of an understanding and growing awareness on the part of the tutor/therapist of the effect of their presence on the members of the group. Art therapists were becoming aware of and curious about new ideas in group dynamics stemming from movements in the USA, such as Encounter, Esalen and their British counterparts, mentioned earlier on. Some embraced the 'growth movement' to such an extent that they temporarily abandoned art therapy though the majority of art therapists were wary of (at least the extremes of) these movements. Those art therapists who were Jungians tended to follow Jung's example and be vociferously against the use of groups in psychotherapy.

The advent of 'performance art' and interactive exercises in the art school curriculum led some artists to try and incorporate these approaches into their work as therapists. Those who became interested in groups found that unconscious themes of the group were often reflected in the images made by group members, allowing a powerful group consciousness to develop. (This phenomenon is known as 'resonance' and is explored further on p. 15.)

In the 1970s, more formal small group sessions developed in which the therapist paid attention to boundaries of time and space – that is, the group would happen at a set time, in a set place each week rather than taking place in an open studio at the convenience of the individuals. These groups had defined membership and a commitment was expected. Sometimes the formation of these groups met with resistance as they aroused strong feelings and lacked the informality of the studio groups.

There are now many art therapists who work with groups but only a few who have formally trained in group psychotherapy and made attempts to synthesise the models. These have mainly been associated with the Art Psychotherapy Unit of Goldsmiths' College which teaches both Art Therapy and Group Psychotherapy courses. The Diploma in Art Psychotherapy at Goldsmiths' uses models of group analytic or interpersonal group therapy as a basis for much of the teaching and experiential work and includes an ongoing large group experience for all art therapy trainees.

Such emphasis had been present in the Goldsmiths' training from its beginning in the mid-1970s. I began my own group analytic training in 1975, just after introducing art therapy to Goldsmiths'. Andrea Gilroy joined the staff a year or so later and with Jenny Waterhouse, began to run group-based art therapy workshops. The group analytic bias increased when Gerry McNeilly, an art therapist, joined the staff in 1979 and shortly after began training at the Institute of Group Analysis (IGA). Later, Joan Woddis and Sally Skaife, both practising art therapists and tutors, trained in group analysis, and Sally Skaife replaced Gerry McNeilly as a workshop leader, making a group-oriented team which also now includes Jane Dudley, a Goldsmiths' art therapy graduate who had many years working experience at the Henderson Therapeutic Community.

Nowadays all art therapy training involves some group work, the main element of which is an art therapy training workshop running throughout the course. This has been declared by the BAAT Training and Education Committee as an essential aspect of the core course requirements, in that art therapists are usually required to work with groups in subsequent employment and they need to have at least basic knowledge and skills in conducting.

RECENT DEVELOPMENTS IN ART THERAPY GROUPS

McNeilly has written eloquently and provocatively about the process he describes as 'group analytic art therapy' which he began to formulate whilst at the IGA in the late 1970s. McNeilly's article entitled 'Directive and non-directive approaches in art therapy' was first published in the American Journal *The Arts and Psychotherapy* in 1983, and later in *Inscape*, in December 1984. McNeilly criticised art therapy practice in which the therapist gave the group emotive themes to work on – rather like a 'recipe book' of themes which he felt only reflected the therapist's defences. His criticisms were partially based on findings from Marion Liebmann's (1979) research : 'A study of structured art therapy groups', which resulted in a booklet called *Art Games and Structures for Groups* (1982) and later a book *Art Therapy for Groups* (1986). I would like now to discuss Liebmann's work so that we can understand the basis of McNeilly's criticism and the ensuing debate.

Liebmann made a survey, as part of her research towards an MA thesis in 1979, of the group work of forty art therapists, and she found that most of the groups had a similar format. She describes this in a chapter written in 1984 (in Dalley, 1984: 160–1) as being composed of an *introduction* followed by an *activity* (the art making process) and then by *discussion*. Thus the groups are highly structured. Under 'introduction' is included welcome to new members, setting boundaries, re-capping on previous sessions, sometimes a physical warm-up. Then:

> The main activity or theme for the session is then introduced. Usually the therapist chooses the activity, according to what has gone on in previous sessions, or the issues that are important at that time. Groups which have been together for some time often play a significant part in choosing the activity for a particular session, and also take on more responsibility in other ways, helping new members, for example.
>
> (in Dalley, 1984: 160)

The 'activity' Liebmann says, usually takes about half the available time:

> Art therapists have to decide to what extent they will participate at this stage. This decision depends on several factors, such as personal philosophy and orientation of the therapist, the kind of group, and the particular activity. Some therapists do join in, because it helps to break down

barriers – if they are asking group members to reveal themselves, then participation by the therapist facilitates this process within the group.

(in Dalley, 1984: 161; see Yalom, 1985: 216–26 for a discussion of the advantages and pitfalls of therapist 'transparency')

The discussion usually takes the second half of the session and sometimes each person has a share of the time available, or contributes to the discussion of one or two paintings; or relates how they felt during a group painting. Liebmann comments that there are many ways of discussing the art products according to the philosophy and theoretical orientation of the therapist, the setting and the particular group.

Liebmann later introduced the concept of 'games' and drew attention to the literature on games of all sorts for groups which are concerned with enhancing people's experience of themselves and others. She pointed out that in the sphere of 'personal growth' a game is any activity which is based on rules that define the framework of that activity and can be used to play. The rules are flexible enough to be interpreted in different ways to allow for many levels of response and the rules can be changed by agreement of the participants. A game constitutes a 'real-life' situation in microcosm and provides a 'parallel frame of reference which operates alongside "real life" but does not become confused with it' (in Dalley, 1984: 163).

She gives several case examples of art therapy groups, including those using games. She describes groups in an alcoholics unit, a women's group in a day hospital, a one-day workshop with a community group, at a day centre for ex-offenders, a peace conference and on an art therapy course. In all these groups, the conductor introduced the group, sometimes by suggesting a warm-up, and directed the activity.

Liebmann ended her chapter 'Art games and group structures':

Using art therapy games and structured activities draws on expertise in art therapy, groups and games and it remains the responsibility of the therapist to make the right choices for the particular group and context, and to learn with the group.

(in Dalley, 1984: 171)

In criticising the approach of what appeared from Liebmann's research to be that of a large number of art therapists, including Liebmann herself, McNeilly described how he too had previously had the aim in a group of giving them a course of direction by setting themes:

Often these themes were derived from intense emotional experiences such as love, hate, dependence, independence. On these occasions the focus became conflicts arising from such polarities. Variations on the theme illuminated the individual's difficulties in dealing with such problems and finding solutions.

(1984: 7)

McNeilly felt that such direct suggestions led to a tendency for too powerful feelings to be uncovered too quickly making it difficult for the group member, the group and the therapist to contain and understand the material. Also, the theme might limit the extent to which the group can develop and this, McNeilly suggests, might be a way in which the therapist controls the depth the group goes to. He criticises the literature on theme-centred art therapy groups as lacking any exploration of interpersonal relationships:

> What occurs in the majority of theme centred groups is a didactic process between separate members and the therapist . . . In this process the therapist is seen as the provider or good mother who gives all the goodies. The therapist has here fallen into a dependency basic assumption from the start. He/she has agreed to feed the group and let it depend on him/her like a mother.
>
> (McNeilly, 1984: 7)

In the non-directive approach, which McNeilly termed 'group analytic', themes do emerge but over a period of time:

> Themes on the whole are more subtle in their development, and may be stronger and more dynamic as their emergence has not been through a direct demand. A synchronistic process may be seen through the production of two or more of the same, or closely related symbols by members of the group. Also in such an approach one can focus on the universality in the group and its symbolic life.
>
> (1984: 8)

Yalom's comments on anti-therapeutic norms (1985: 190–1) back up this criticism in that artwork is often discussed by members 'taking turns' or being pressured into premature self-disclosure by being required to work on a theme which may be, for some, too highly emotive at that moment in the group; or entering into what Yalom calls the 'Can you top this?' format in which members engage in a 'spiraling orgy of self-disclosure or a tightly knit, closed pattern that excludes outlying members and does not welcome new ones' (1985: 191).

McNeilly's article was strongly criticised, perhaps not surprisingly given that many art therapists were using a theme-centred approach. Roy Thornton (1985: 23–4), and a group of art therapists in the Bristol area, including Marian Liebmann, offered another view. Thornton argued:

> Does it not occur [to McNeilly] that themes can be used with careful thought for clinically based purposes, as suggestions, quite free of obligation, in full knowledge of transference issues, not evasively, but to

create intensity, and that the technique is supported by ample evidence of fruitful, wide ranging interchanges full of meaning, with good effect.

(1985: 23)

Thornton had himself spent a year at the Institute of Group Analysis but was not persuaded to commit himself to the group analytic method. He reports being struck by the 'awful slowness of the approach, and the high proportion of people who dropped out' (p. 23). He disagreed that the use of themes was inevitably harmful but acknowledged that a 'themes-off-the-shelf' approach in the hands of a novice could be. He concludes that direction that was openly acknowledged, rather than implicit, required a high degree of sophistication in understanding and action and a high degree of effective compassion and was certainly not an easy option. He agreed that it was possible for a therapist to stand in the way of his or her availability for transference and impose their own personality by using techniques defensively. On the other hand, it was possible to be skilled in the 'knowing use of oneself and one's technique, awake to both the economic value of themes and yet their inherent dangers: and so to avoid using these skills could be, paradoxically, the very cop out we are being invited to adopt' (p. 25).

Wadeson, although not directly participating in this 'British' debate, has the following to contribute:

The most significant question regarding structured art activities (including guided imagery) is not what to use, but whether and when one should use them at all. Recently I sat in on a class of about 20 art therapists and a few art therapy students. The group went 'round' three times, each telling of an art therapy technique he or she used. In a short time, we had heard about 60 techniques. Most people took notes. The student next to me titled hers, 'Recipes for Art Therapy'.

Art therapy isn't a piece of cake. An art therapist isn't there to provide projects. If she trusts the power of imagery and the healing forces within her client, she will allow her groups to flow naturally and organically. She will trust herself to be sensitive to their emergence so that she can foster their exploration and encourage the growth potential of the art therapy group and its individual members.

(Wadeson, 1980: 158)

The debate has continued, with polarisation appearing to have lessened in favour of more considered discussion of the role that the image-making process can play within group art therapy.

It is interesting to consider why so many art therapists – at the least the cross-section that Liebmann interviewed – chose to run their groups on what seems to be a therapist-led model. It may simply be that, as her research was carried out in the mid-1970s, this was the model they inherited from non-group trained tutors at college, or had absorbed from occupational therapy colleagues' 'projective art' groups. A few words on the latter: these groups depended upon the therapist presenting an emotive theme to which the patients were expected to respond visually and then discuss in the group. Theoretically the model seems to derive from psychological tests which use images (Thematic Apperception Test, Rorschach, etc.)[1] except that the patient is expected to 'project' his or her emotional response through a personal image rather than responding to a given image. It also may derive from experience of a once-common practice in art lessons at school, where the art teacher gave the class a theme (e.g. Christmas) and during the course of the lesson would walk around the class commenting on the progress of the painting. There was no discussion of the psychological meaning of the resulting images, however, unless the children happened to be attending a 'special school' where art classes sometimes had a 'therapeutic' flavour.

It is hardly surprising, given the lack of group training, that art therapists adhered to a highly structured model, in which the group process could be monitored and controlled. When group interaction is combined with image-making and the group process takes control, very powerful forces are unleashed. Without the confidence that a thorough training and experience in group dynamics should impart, art therapists were probably wise to try and 'keep the lid on'. They were often working with severely damaged people for whom interaction might present a high level of anxiety – perhaps too high to handle. Nevertheless, the criticism McNeilly made was timely as it drew attention to what might have become a 'habit' in conducting groups rather than a seriously considered and theoretically sound approach, based on the patients' ability to participate and on recognition of the therapist's own level of skill. It also drew people's attention to the fact that setting themes could be damaging in certain situations.

In 1987 McNeilly wrote 'Further contributions to group analytic art therapy' in which he expanded on his previous controversial 'Directive and non-directive approaches'. In this paper, McNeilly related his work closely to Foulkes's 'A basic law of group dynamics' (1983: 29–30). McNeilly says that in applying Foulkes's work to group analytic art therapy, the merits lay in the high level of involvement with the whole learning process, with the interchanging of members' positions in the group. He pointed out that he had been criticised for appearing to give the artwork a secondary or incidental position or value but in fact this was not so. Rather, he did not 'chase the in-depth symbolic nature of the individual image' and 'may not comment on some of the pictures'. Yet, as Foulkes had pointed out, the individual was a 'nodal' point in the system and therefore either an interpretation of the collective imagery or an individual interpretation would resonate with all on different levels. However, he concluded, communication was more important than interpretation.

By this time, McNeilly seems to have moved rather towards the 'inter-active' pole in emphasising the interactions between members in the here-and-now. He also concedes that there may be groups of people for whom the analytical approach would not be beneficial 'if applied in its purest form, although I believe many of Foulkes' principles may be used in any group' (1987: 9). He mentions mentally handicapped people, hyperactive children, certain adolescent groups, severe psychopaths and long-stay psychiatric patients as needing higher levels of structure and boundary, thus calling for: 'greater directive and teaching input from the leader, as an *apparent* lack of direction by a leader tends to stir up insecurity and bring intra-psychic processes more to the fore' (1987: 9).

In his earlier article (1984), McNeilly had introduced the concept of 'resonance' which was elaborated by Roberts (1985). The term 'resonance' is an analogical term derived from the science of acoustics and defined as the reinforcement or prolongation of sound by reflection or synchronous vibration. According to analytic theory, a deep unconscious frame of reference is laid down in the first five years of life and predetermines associative responses from then on. A person may become 'fixated' or 'regressed' and on entering a therapeutic group, becomes associated with others functioning at different levels of the psycho-sexual scale. Each member in the group will then show a tendency to reverberate or resonate to any group event according to the level at which he is set (Foulkes and Anthony, 1965: 152). The term is used by them to describe a group process which appears to be determined by two factors: the interactions between people and the reactions of individual people to the current theme of the group. Foulkes spoke of a 'chain of resonances' indicating the consecutive manner in which the 'resonant' material emerged. In an art group, however, members express themselves through images simultaneously and so the resulting artworks become available as tangible representations of what was happening simultaneously in all the members (Roberts, 1985: 17).

Resonance occurs when each member of a group responds to a stimulating input (such as the impending group break) so that the group as a whole becomes highly charged with energy. Very powerful emotions may be evoked – for example, a theme of separation may emerge in a group, evoking powerful responses in each member who produces his or her own material relevant to separation or avoidance of it. Thus the member 'resonates' to the group theme at his or her natural frequency (Roberts, 1985: 17). The paper draws attention to a phenomenon which Roberts had noted from his close observation of or participation in several art therapy groups, namely, that half or more of the members spontaneously produced a picture or article making clear reference to a single theme. This was, however, a theme which had emerged through the group process as opposed to being offered by the conductor at the beginning (see Case Example No. 10, pp. 133–5).

In the same issue of *Inscape* in which McNeilly developed his group analytic approach (1987), Helen Greenwood, an art therapist, and Geoff Layton, a community psychiatrist described one of the art therapy groups they were conducting in a day centre. This was a once-weekly group with eight patients, all of whom had suffered major psychiatric disorders and many of whom had been readmitted several times to hospital. They set a regular time (12 hours) and place for the session, using a large room with comfortable chairs, tables that needed to be erected, art materials – paper, paint and clay. This group was structured and the art therapist encouraged group members to select paper and begin an exploration of materials. Themes were

> intermittently introduced by the therapists with caution that the group did not depend on a suggested theme. These themes were non-threatening. An example could be 'water', giving a wide scope of images from a dripping tap, to a raging waterfall, a tranquil lake or the expanse of the ocean.
>
> (Greenwood and Layton, 1987: 13)

When everyone had finished drawing they went to sit in armchairs with the pictures in front of them on the floor and about fifty minutes was spent in verbal discussion. Common themes evolved in discussion which were pursued verbally.

A culture developed in the group, which was as follows: the start of the session developed into a 5 to 10-minute chat during which time themes spontaneously emerged which were taken up as the subject for exploration in art or sometimes group members presented a theme that they had thought about during the week. They found that the theme gave a focus for the projection of anxieties and that the group members would suggest difficult and threatening themes and scorn those non-threatening ones previously suggested by the therapists (1987: 14).

They make the point that by personal choice they would not work with themes, preferring a more spontaneous approach. They felt, however, that this might increase anxiety and confusion and lead to further disintegration in this group of potentially psychotic patients (p. 14). There seems to be disagreement here with Yalom's point (and McNeilly's) that the setting of themes might actually increase anxiety and certainly lead to pressure for premature self-disclosure. Rather, it appears that themes in an art therapy group are generally considered as a way of *containing* anxiety (within the art object) and giving a focus for its projection.

The authors refer to W.R. Bion's *Learning from Experience* (1962). There are three phases – projection, digestion and re-introjection in the process of *containment* which may be fulfilled within the act of art making. The authors say:

Using Bion's concept of containment when we consider what happens in the process of art therapy in this group, it is as if material is projected and given some form in the art product. This is worked with in the art process itself, and also by the group in the verbal discussion. When the group and the therapists become the container, the projected material, the picture, is acknowledged and explored, and then work is done to relate this to the artist with reference to previous artwork, and also to the group. Once the projected material can be seen in the context of a structure, symbolising internal mechanisms, then it can be re-introjected, acknowledged and accepted as part of one's self.

(Greenwood and Layton, 1987: 16)

Thus although Greenwood and Layton use a broadly 'theme-centred' approach, they also make use of interpersonal or interactive models – especially in the degree to which they become transparent by engaging in the art-making process themselves, and they draw on insights from group analysis to understand the material.

If we accept that the art object can act as a container for strong and even unacceptable emotions, it may be that there is less 'danger' (i.e. from premature self-disclosure, etc.) in using themes in an art therapy group, given that the art object can remain exactly as that – i.e. it need not be talked about. However, there is usually pressure to disclose, especially if the group time is structured to include discussion.

The pressure to describe feelings in words is one which most of us experience in groups, even art therapy groups which are described as 'non-verbal'. David Maclagan (1985) writes that according to what he calls the 'mythology' of art therapy, there is the assumption that through sponta-neous painting and drawing a person can relax their conscious controls and enter directly into contact with unconscious material. He says that even the choice of techniques: big brushes, sloppy paint and other devices to eliminate skill, must aim at spontaneity without which it will not be possible for unconscious processes to come through. Some art therapists, he says, believe that the image must be protected and not reflected upon too consciously for fear of disturbing 'the fragile balance between the voluntary and involuntary'. There is a strong anti-verbal tradition in art therapy which regards explanation or interpretation with extreme suspicion. He asks, then, how can art therapy play anything other than a compensatory (or possibly subversive) role in a programme based on group psychotherapy?

Maclagan says that he makes a basic assumption that art therapy is a kind of 'net' for images and that the images have meaning and value not only for the person who created them but also for the group. The images do not have to be aesthetically pleasing: they may in fact be chaotic, aggressive, unstable or impersonal or contain 'psychotic' features. The image has to be looked at and accepted for what it is, firstly by the person who made it. The structure of the art therapy group provides a frame within which feelings and fantasies can be discovered and communicated without being deperso-nalised. Maclagan continues, commenting that psychotherapy is 'enormously dependent upon the capacity to allow symbolisation and relax the boundaries of common sense':

> Dealing with non-verbal imagery, or rather with the translation between non-verbal and verbal, throws this issue into sharp relief: the literalness, concreteness and rationalisation of some patients appears in all its rigidity, not only in the way in which they represent their feelings but in the degree to which they can accept alternative readings of their images.
>
> (Maclagan, 1985: 8)

I take Maclagan to mean that the patients are seeking a direct rendering of words into images and vice versa. In other words, not being able, or willing, to let the images have a life of their own, or to 'free associate' to them.

Working within a therapeutic community, where the art therapy group is unusual in containing material objects which are loaded with metaphoric and symbolic meaning has its problems: in particular, the question of how to use the material from art therapy within the community. There is the problem of continuity between one week's group and the next and what Maclagan refers to as the 'lizard's tail' syndrome, whereby powerful and significant images are effectively cast off and left behind. Wadeson also comments on the image that gets 'left behind' (by 'conventional group therapy' she means verbal interactive groups):

> Although in conventional group therapy sessions there may be material that gets postponed due to lack of time, such issues aren't usually recognized in such a way as to incur the frustration that an unexplained, provocative picture does. In conventional group therapy, at any particular session, some members may be relatively passive or simply reactive to others rather than introducing issues of their own. When each member creates an art expression, however, each introduces material, so there is much out on the table, so to speak. In another respect, this phenomenon is advantageous in groups with members who otherwise are withdrawn. Through their art productions, they capture the group's attention, which helps to integrate them into the group.
>
> (1980: 238)

I am not clear why this is such a problem because in a long-term group the material will still be available for use by the individual and the group whenever it wishes. There may be a difference though in the fact that all the images are 'out' and available and may have strong projective potential. Group members have to carry these visual projections with them until the next session.

Wadeson (1987: 147–8) mentions that an important aspect of the utilisation of art in group therapy is its important place not only in reflecting group process, as previously described, but in its advancing group process. This advancement occurs simultaneously with the sort of reflection that group images provide. For example, when group members draw pictures of the group, awareness becomes magnified. Each person has shared his or her view; common constellations are identified; different perceptions are recognised; feelings about the group are communicated; each member has access to the position he or she holds in every member's conception of the group. Usually there has been risk in divulging these perceptions. All this information and sharing of feeling adds substantially to the growth of the group. As a result, the group ends the session in a far different (psychological) place from where it began.

When coming across a group which is apparently so permissive and tolerant of the bizarre and irrational, staff and patients may become suspicious of what is going on. Participants may be 'playing', making a mess of the room, and laughter and physical activity (such as lying on the floor to be drawn, pounding clay, building structures) are commonplace. I have encountered this suspicion, or anxiety perhaps, myself when working within the therapeutic community structure and within institutions where art therapy is a very new modality. It is one which produces objects and images which are difficult to 'read' by those outside the group. It is essential that good relations between the conductor of the art therapy group and the other staff are fostered if art therapy is not to go out to the margins and be dismissed as 'not really part of the work'.

THE POSITION TODAY

In the special edition of *Group Analysis* 'Group Analysis and the Arts Therapies' (Sept. 1990) it became clear that the approach of group analytic or group interactive art therapy was being modified to suit a wide range of client groups from long-stay mentally handicapped people (Strand, 1990), to women with eating disorders (Levens, 1990), and day centre clients (McNeilly, 1990).

Strand points out that it is easy to reinforce the notion of dependency and childishness among people with mental handicaps if the focus is always on staff teaching skills and setting standards which the clients have to fulfil. She draws attention to the lack of opportunities for clients to express emotions, especially anger and frustration, in behavioural programmes which stress social conformity. She established a closed art group of seven clients which met weekly for 1 hour and 45 minutes. All the clients had spent most of their lives in care and some had been in that particular hospital from childhood. They were all verbal.

Strand and her co-therapist (also an art therapist) saw their role as encouraging members to communicate with each other and: 'to learn that our expectations of them were not to please us but concerned with their recognizing their own needs and emotions' (1990: 259). It was a difficult shift as the members had tended to direct all questions and responses to the conductors. The group was structured so that the first hour was spent in image-making and the remaining 45 minutes in discussion. As members became familiar with the structure, the conductors observed a greater degree of interaction. There was a high level of motivation to show work and gain the attention of the group.

The fact that the group was closed established it as a significant event in the week. It provided a sense of consistency and continuity in an institution which had a high staff turnover and where residents were to some degree at the mercy of external events – i.e. being moved to different wards and into different programmes. Thus it was difficult to form and retain close relationships.

Strand saw one of the most important elements in this interactive art therapy group as enabling members to take responsibility for their own images and for their own emotional responses. One very powerful theme which emerged from the group was that of loss: of family or friends; a sense of being rejected and abandoned; the realisation of being 'different' and not 'normal'; the fear of death. Feelings associated with loss had little opportunity for expression in the day-to-day lives of the residents. Through the art therapy and interactive process, they were able to acknowledge sadness and loneliness. They were not obliged to 'keep cheerful'.

This article is a most important contribution to the development of group interactive art therapy. It shows trust and confidence in these long-stay, institutionalised residents and great sensitivity to their situation. Although verbal, their articulation was limited, and the image-making process provided an essential 'key' to communication. It is to be hoped that Strand's article will stimulate other art therapists working with people with mental handicaps – either in the few remaining long-stay institutions or in the community – to introduce such groups.

It is clear that both group psychotherapy and art therapy are flexible modalities, able to be adapted in work with people whose emotional needs are often dismissed in favour of more rigid behavioural models (see Tipple, 1992 for further useful information).

Having explored some of the ways in which art therapists have worked with groups from the 1940s up to the present, I will outline in the following chapter the theoretical approach to groups which is known as 'interpersonal' or 'interactive' group psychotherapy.

NOTE

1 The Rorschach ink blots and the Thematic Apperception Test elicit imaginal productions which may be rated in terms of their originality as well as in terms of their personal meaning to the subject. They are, of course, far from 'objective'. For further information see Barron (1968).

Chapter 2

Interactive group psychotherapy

The interactive or interpersonal approach to psychotherapy derives from the work of the neo-Freudians and in particular Harry Stack Sullivan (1953). Sullivan believed that an individual's history influences every moment of his life, because it provides a dynamic structure and definition of his experiences. He saw anxiety as arising from threats to an individual's self-esteem. The individual uses well-tried defences to deal with these threats. Stack Sullivan did not agree with Freud's idea that the basic personality structure was laid down in early childhood: rather he felt it developed, through interaction with significant others, right through to adulthood and was therefore open to change. A person's psychological growth, then, depends on a concept of the self which is largely based on how a person experiences himself in relation to others (see Ratigan and Aveline, 1988: 47).

A very informative account of group interactive psychotherapy is given by Yalom (1975) and the model is well described by Ratigan and Aveline in 'Group Psychotherapy in Britain' (1988: 43–64) and several therapeutic features of the model are explored by Bloch and Crouch (1985). I shall not try to reproduce their work in this chapter, but merely attempt to highlight some of the points that they make. I would recommend a thorough reading of these sources for further elucidation of history, theory and practice of the model.

Group interactive psychotherapy focusses on the actions, reactions and characteristic patterns of interaction which constrain people in their everyday lives and for which help in modifying is sought in the group (Ratigan and Aveline, 1988: 45). A fundamental of the approach is that each person constructs an individual inner world which is continuously being reconstructed through interactions with others and which determines that person's view of himself and others and affects expectations of others. In group therapy, the individual gradually realises how inner assumptions may determine the patterns of interaction that develop. Exploration of these patterns and willingness to modify them in the safety of the group enables the person to try out new ways of relating in the 'outside world'. Clearly, then, the model places the main source of change in the interaction between group members and depends upon the participants learning from each other.

There are five concepts central to the interpersonal approach. These are explicated in existential philosophy and psychology and therein, the authors suggest, lies the difference between this approach and analytically-oriented group psychotherapy. The concepts are as follows:

1 Human actions are not predetermined; freedom is part of the human condition.
2 The corollary of this is the importance of choice in human life.
3 It is essential to take responsibility for one's actions.
4 Death is inevitable; but the fact that we shall all die can paradoxically give meaning to life.
5 We are each engaged in a creative search for individual patterns that will give meaning to our existence (Ratigan and Aveline, 1988: 45).

The concepts of responsibility, freedom and choice are central to the interactive model. The approach provides:

> a clinical context where group members can move from being trapped in a personal world view in which they are passive victims of cruel circumstance to a self-formed one where they can take more responsibility for their lives, relationships, symptoms and difficulties. The central therapeutic effect is not just an intellectual appreciation of an active world view but a lived experience in the group of enlarged freedom through experiences of new personal acts or refraining from maladaptive acts. This is not an absolute freedom but a tension towards a greater freedom within the context of a person's circumstances.
>
> (Ratigan and Aveline, 1988: 46)

Each member, then, is expected to take responsibility for his or her own participation in the learning experience of the group, to have a sense of their own influence on events and not see themselves as passive victims of circumstances. Members do not simply talk about their difficulties in the group but actually reveal them through their here-and-now behaviour. In this model, the 'here-and-now' is where the therapy takes place and 'reporting' on past experiences is discouraged. Disclosure does, however, take place: that is, revelation of 'secrets' or significant events from the past and present outside the group and this may be important in understanding the behaviour of that individual in the group. The act of disclosing releases tension, usually brings the member closer to others and enables defences to be lowered and eventually dropped (see Case Example No. 8, pp. 126-9).

Feedback from members of the group illuminates aspects of the self which have become obvious to others but which are not recognised by oneself. The emphasis in an interactive group is on members giving accurate feedback and owning their feelings (Ratigan and Aveline, 1988: 49). Feedback is often hard to take, despite being apparently desired by members, but to be effective it has to be well timed and preferably delivered with some sensitivity for it is useless if the member is unable to hear or to deal with it.

The preparedness of members to take risks – i.e. to put themselves in an exposed position by behaving differently from usual – is essential to this model's effectiveness. I sometimes refer to the group as a 'rehearsal ground' where ways of relating may be tried out without fear of ridicule or retaliation. If members feel safe enough to 'be themselves' or in other words to acknowledge the thoughts and feelings they are really having as opposed to those they feel they *should* be having, then they will demonstrate the patterns of behaviour which have led them to therapy and in turn receive assistance in changing these patterns. Members do, however, tend to avoid the 'here-and-now' relationships initially, in favour of talking about life outside the group, as these inter-group relationships can be powerful and even frightening for some members, and most people have not learned to be direct about what they are thinking and feeling. Yet these relationships can be the most therapeutic.

In an interactive group, the process of *projection* involves group members having feelings and making assumptions about other members which are not based on their here-and-now experience. For example, one member experiences another as his stern father and makes assumptions about that person's feelings towards him. *Mirroring* entails a member having strong feelings and emotions about another's behaviour which is in fact an aspect of theirs. Projection and mirroring are often accompanied by *splitting* – i.e. by experiencing a group member, the conductor or the whole group as all good or all bad; and scapegoating, when the group tries to put all its difficulties onto one member and to get rid of them (see Case Example No. 11, pp. 136–44). The members' tendency to distort their perceptions of others (parataxic distortions) provides valuable material for the group to work on.

Another phenomenon of these groups is *projective identification*, which can result in one member projecting their own (but actually disowned) attributes onto another, towards whom they feel 'an uncanny attraction-repulsion' (Yalom, 1985: 354) These attributes are projected strongly *into* the other person, so that that person's behaviour begins to change. For example, murderous feelings may be projected so that the other person begins to feel murderous, whereas the projector has no awareness of such a feeling.

The group itself, as a social microcosm, also gets into patterns of behaviour as if it were an individual. According to Ezriel (1950) the group may take up a 'required' relationship with the conductor or with each other, which safeguards them from the 'avoided' relationship which they fear may in turn lead to a 'calamitous' relationship. For example, the group may never challenge the conductor lest he or she should become angry and terminate the group or retaliate in some other way. It is important for the conductor to understand when these processes are in action and to comment on them. Members may then learn to make such connections themselves, later on.

If we accept that patterns of behaviour are learned and that it is possible to unlearn or relearn more effective or rewarding ways of being, then there is much to be learned from interpersonal interaction within the boundaries of a group.

Bloch and Crouch (1985: 68) state:

> there is a fundamental therapeutic factor which is a direct consequence of interaction, variously labelled as interpersonal learning and learning from interpersonal action. As these labels imply, we are concerned with a learning process in which the emphasis is on learning from actual experience; more specifically from new efforts – tantamount to experimentation – at relating to others.

They point out that the early pioneers of group therapy were 'virtually oblivious' to the potential advantages of promoting interaction either between group members themselves or between members and the therapists. With the application in the 1930s of the psychoanalytical model to groups, interaction did begin to occupy a prominent place but this was largely confined to the relationships that evolved between the analyst and each patient. In other words, group treatment was regarded as comparable to individual analysis, with attention being paid to the analysis of transference. The dimensions of transference were substantially wider than obtained in classical psychoanalysis as it was possible for a patient to become strongly attached not only to the therapist but to other group members and the group as a whole. A separate therapeutic factor, interaction, was considered by Corsini and Rosenberg (writing in 1955) as the most difficult factor to understand and classify. They produced a limited definition which Bloch and Crouch suggest was not surprising as they were relying on scattered writings, mainly from the 1940s:

> Clinicians were then only beginning to perceive that relating between group members, including the therapist, might carry therapeutic potential above and beyond transference. Such terms as interaction, relationship, contact with others, and interstimulation had made their appearance but their conceptual basis was ill-understood and rudimentary.
>
> (1985: 69)

In the 1950s, representatives of the humanistic psychology and human potential movement – e.g. H. Stack Sullivan, Karen Horney and Erich Fromm emphasised interpersonal issues and the subject of interaction was:

tackled head on and its qualities identified. At the same time, the strict Freudian mould that had been applied to groups began to soften. Transference was not the sole form of relating in group therapy; other forms existed alongside it and were of equivalent importance.

(1985: 69–70)

Irving Yalom, whose work I have already referred to, developed concepts of interpersonal learning which are thoroughly and clearly outlined in his book, *The Theory and Practice of Group Psychotherapy*, first published in 1975. According to Yalom, the group provides a forum in which the patient can explore and develop his relationships with others, resulting in greater trust and improved social skills. Yalom based his theory of interpersonal learning on Stack Sullivan's interpersonal theory of psychiatry. He maintained that psychiatric symptoms and problems originate in and express themselves as disturbed interpersonal relationships. Yalom emphasises two concepts: (a) the group as a social microcosm and (b) the corrective emotional experience.

'Social microcosm' refers to a group process which resembles customary everyday functioning, in which patients tend to behave in their usual maladaptive way. It is by observing and drawing attention to these behaviour patterns in the group that the therapist and other group members can have a 'corrective emotional experience', thus helping each other to change. This process has been summarised by Bloch and Crouch as follows:

> the patient takes the risk, emboldened by the group's supportive structure, of expressing some strong emotion to one or more group members, including, perhaps, the therapist. Within the context of the here-and-now, the protagonist is able to reflect on the emotional experience he has undergone and to become aware, with the aid of fellow-members, how appropriate his reactions were. This awareness paves the way for an improvement in interpersonal relating.

(1985: 77)

In summary then, the interactive model proposes that:

1 The patient's symptoms are derived from disturbed interpersonal relationships, probably at a very early level. These symptoms usually adversely affect interpersonal functioning and the major presenting problem is therefore difficulty in relating to others.
2 The therapist promotes a climate in which the patient can learn about and understand those patterns of behaviour which are causing distress.
3 Awareness leads to the possibility of change. This is more likely to happen if the patient is committed to the group, that is, attends regularly and participates, and is willing to take risks.
4 The patient experiments with new behaviour in the group. Feedback from

therapist and other group members as well as self-observation enables him to judge the effectiveness of his efforts.

5 The new behaviour is tried out by the patient – with family, friends, workmates, etc., and the results reported back to the group.

If all goes well:

An 'adaptive spiral' is set up which severs the previous circular link between symptoms and disturbed relationships. More adaptive interpersonal behaviour generates greater self-esteem. The possibility for further rewarding relationships is encouraging and boosts self-esteem, promoting yet more change.

(Bloch and Crouch, 1985: 78)

Thompson and Khan (1988: 75) consider that the patient tries to recreate in the group the original 'network' of relationships in which the conflict was first experienced, using different individuals, including the leader, to represent different protagonists. They also point out that the group itself might symbolise a person, an idea or an object or situation – for example, mother. The roles that the patients take up might resemble those in their original family and thus the whole network is transferred onto the group. They suggest that the language used to describe the effect of these transferred relationships will vary according to whichever theory is being used. So the pattern of the communications in the group will be influenced in some way by the theoretical position which the group leader holds.

In this model, then, it is not considered necessary for the patient to delve into their past history to try and understand why they are like they are, but they are encouraged to learn to observe their own patterns of behaviour in the group, their effect on others and how the patterns serve a purpose. In this sense, there is a difference between the analytic and interactional theoretical schools, although many therapists use elements of both. The main difference seems to be that the group analyst encourages the patient to acquire insight through the examination of transference within the framework of emotional interaction. The interactionalist emphasises reciprocal action or influence between members and argues that interaction is the chief agent for change.

In both schools the therapist is regarded as a central figure but the interactionalist views him or herself as a relatively transparent catalyst and model, whereas the analyst sees themself as an opaque, neutral observer. The interactionalist works mainly in the present; the analyst makes liberal use of historical data and the 'there-and-then'. The interactionalist puts much emphasis on the group experience being a positive one from the outset whereas the analyst believes that resistance to learning must first be removed before patients are capable of benefiting from positive experience.

Not all workers see much difference between group analytic and group interactive models. For example, Cohn (1969), while conceding that differences do exist between analytic and experiential (or interactive) models, especially in relation to the therapist's role and the temporal framework, does not believe they constitute a dichotomy. She considers that the therapeutic process involves both interactional here-and-now experience plus the there-and-then of past and future.

Bloch and Crouch point out that it may seem that Cohn wants to have her cake and eat it:

> For an analytically oriented therapist to act as transparently as an experiential therapist and continue to make interpretations about transference is a tall order both clinically and theoretically. We suspect that Durkin comes closer to the truth than Cohn when she contends that despite any overlap, the nature of the therapist–patient relationship in the two approaches differs markedly. But the question then arises as to whether aspects of each may be moulded into a completely new theory, a theory in which interaction retains a prominent place.
>
> (1985: 80)

From my reading of case studies by group analytic psychotherapists, I am convinced that in practice there is often as much overlap as Cohn suggests.

Cohn's work is interesting and relevant to this book in that she was a pioneer in the area of theme-centred interactive group psychotherapy. Her interest began when she initiated a workshop in countertransference which was designed for the study and treatment of countertransference through self-analysis, in a workshop setting. She found that the therapist who revealed their relationship with the patient to the group through free associations stimulated interactional responses in their listeners, to useful effect. Cohn developed other workshops with a single theme as a result of this initial experiment and extended these to a wide group of participants, including the business community. Some of her themes were directly related to major news events, such as the murder of President Kennedy, and she incorporated people's responses to this event into her workshops.

Cohn would sometimes ask patients to be silent at the beginning of the workshop and concentrate on the given theme and on the feelings it aroused. A specific example might be: choose one of the people in the group and fantasise in silence something important you might say to him. Cohn reported that, as a result of this reflection in silence, many communications proved to be intuitive and meaningful to the receiver of the message. (We may note that the beginning of an art therapy group is often characterised by people working on their images in silence.)

Cohn felt that theme-centred groups moved back and forth between intellectual considerations and emotional experiences, between intrapsychic and interpersonal involvements and intra-group and outside world phenomena, and between strict adherence to the theme and free associations and interactions. In the case studies which illustrate some of the theoretical points in this book, I have tried to show how this is a feature of the interactive art therapy group where an open-ended theme is presented and from which free association develops (see Case Examples 6, 7, 8 and 11).

Ruitenbeek (1970: 21) comments on the variations on Cohn's work which started appearing in the late 1960s. One of these was the time-limited, theme-centred group. One conductor, Buchanan, used devices such as playing music, reciting poetry, etc. so that participants would use their sensory equipment, intuition and perceptiveness of others. The introduction of a theme to be realised through art materials has already been discussed in Chapter 1 and as we have seen, is or was the most usual way of conducting an art therapy group.

Ruitenbeek suggests that the presentation of a single theme[1] might be attractive for contemporary patients:

> They live in a fragmented society and it often seems difficult for them to place all of their problems in a personal and societal context. The attack by a group on a single problem might at least provide the patient with some focus and perhaps offer him a small perspective in his own confused life.
>
> (1970: 213)

Astrachan (1970) who, rather like Cohn is another 'synthesiser', proposes that all the major models of group therapy which could be defined as 'leader-centred' and stress the relationship between the therapist and members, and therapist and group as a whole, neglect important interactional patterns. In the patient–therapist model, the therapist's behaviour prevents a peer culture developing, so while patients may learn about the relationships to authority they miss out on improving relationships with peers. Conversely, in the member to member model, more effective interpersonal relationships may develop but dealing with authority figures will not be adequately tackled.

Astrachan claims that a model based on general systems theory would enable therapists to appreciate the many diverse aspects of their role as 'regulatory agents' and be attuned to all parts of the therapy system. They would therefore be well placed to modify their regulatory posture in the light of the system's specific needs at a particular time and to recognise the likely repercussions on the system of the regulatory behaviour they adopt. Among the therapist's tasks would be to define and maintain the boundaries of therapy – to decide what is pertinent for the group's agenda, what is in the group and what is outside it, and how patients relate to each other. The therapist would thus attend to all systems relevant to the patient and not only the therapy one – e.g. the patient's work, marriage, relationship with parents, relationship with a wider social circle, and to social and political events. In adopting a systems approach, the therapist would be flexible in the role as group leader because he or she would not be bound by a segmental view of the therapeutic process *vis-à-vis* the learning that stems from interaction. All forms of interaction would be potentially useful and none would have priority over the rest (Bloch and Crouch, 1985: 80–1)

Bloch and Crouch find Astrachan's arguments persuasive and in his advocacy of general systems theory he is supported by prominent theorists such as Kernberg (1975), Fried (1975), Skynner (1976) and Durkin (1982). His theories are, however, yet to be tested.

Astrachan's proposals for a model based on general systems theory are, I find, very compelling and creative in their attempts to break new ground, or rather to build a new model from the best of the existing interactional models: much as art therapists have tried to do when introducing visual media to a group. Each member brings to the group a social system of which he is part and from which he is only temporarily disconnected while the session is in progress. Exploration of the patient's 'inner' world, its relationship to the 'here-and-now' of the group and to the social system of which the group is part can be very valuable and quite reassuring to individual members.

To give an example, during the week in which ex-prime minister Margaret Thatcher was removed from office, one group attempted to displace me by disparaging everything I said, my approach to conducting the group and so on. They attempted to choose another 'leader', a male who was fairly willing to take on the role. The attacks were quite ferocious, particularly from the men and including one who had always found difficulty in being assertive. I made an observation that perhaps female leaders were in for a rough time from now on. The group spotted the connection – although they had been very deeply involved in the displacement and apparently unaware of any outside influence. They went on to explore how they felt about having me as a female leader and whether they saw me as mother or father. The usually unassertive man said he had never felt comfortable about having a woman 'in charge' and he had suddenly felt a great urge to attack me. The fact that he had done so without actually killing me off was a great relief. He was able to get in touch with fears about women in general and their power over him, which made him very angry and depressed and made him feel like a small child. Some other group members said that they experienced me like a father, as 'men should be in authority'. They also discussed, in dynamic terms, the actual displacement of Mrs Thatcher. This is an example of the 'outside world' being brought in unconsciously by the group, linking up with transference to myself, to people's individual issues with female authority figures, and interaction among members dealing with a change in the group 'system' – i.e. a previously unassertive male actively challenging the leader and a shift in the 'balance of power' in the group.

Agazarian and Peters (1989) have developed a model of interactive theory that makes use of important and relevant aspects of psychoanalysis and group dynamics and links it with systems theory. They draw on Kurt Lewin's field theory (Lewin, 1951) and general systems theory, turning to field theory to describe the process by which the group-as-a-whole emerges from the interaction among individuals. They suggest:

> The major advantage of field theory is that its constructs are compatible with psychoanalytic constructs. But whereas Freud was mainly concerned with motivation and drive, and how motivation explained a person's perception of the world and his behaviour in it, Lewin was mainly concerned with behaviour, and how behaviour could explain a person's perception of the world (and by inference, his motivation). As most of the group-as-a-whole phenomenon is implied by group behaviour, and as none of the group-as-a-whole phenomenon can be explained by individual motivation, field theory and psychoanalytic theory provided us with two different but compatible ways of describing our observations.
>
> (1989: 33)

General systems theory was the second element that contributed to Agazarian and Peters's notion of the 'invisible' group. They suggest that, since systems theory and field theory have a common ancestor in gestalt psychology, systems analysis is compatible with field theory, which in turn is compatible with psychoanalytic theory.

Lewin's theory is important to consider here, especially his proposal that an individual's behaviour can be predicted from knowledge of his 'life space'. Lewin depicted life space as an egg-shaped 'map' that portrayed the individual in interaction with his perceived environment:

> to understand an individual's life space is to understand his goals, the tension system related to the goal, the barriers between him and his goal, and the probable next step that he will take along his path to his goal. Driving forces are the applications of energy moving him towards the goal, and restraining forces are those quantums of energy that serve to restrain him from reaching his goal. Lewin stated that to draw an accurate picture of an individual's life space was to be able to predict his next behaviour.
>
> (Agazarian and Peters, 1989: 34)

The life space definition, when applied to the individual perspective, serves to illustrate some important dynamics. Agazarian and Peters argue that in the group situation, the interactions of the members create the environment within which they continue to interact. Thus, for group members, their behaviour is a function of their particular psychodynamics, their outside socialising experience, the resultant set of selective perception tendencies plus that group culture of which they are a part. For the therapist, there is an extra factor explaining behaviour, which is the theoretical model through which the therapist is selectively perceiving. So the therapist's behaviour in a group is a function of the same factors that govern member's behaviour plus his or her ability to cognitively structure the group phenomena through his theoretical discipline, training and experience (Agazarian and Peters, 1989: 37).

Agazarian and Peters (1989: 40) make an interesting point about defining a system in relationship to its environment (of which it is a component sub-system). Such a definition, they say, depends on what you want to understand. If, for example, one is talking about a group in relationship to the group's environment, such as a psychotherapy group in a clinic, then the group can be usefully talked about as a sub-system of its environment: transactions from the clinic affect the group and vice versa. It is valuable in this case to think about transactions across the boundary (input and output relations between the group and the clinic) and to pay close attention to the character of the boundaries. But if you are interested in exploring the relationship between the group and its members, then you will talk about the input and output relationships between the group as a system and the individual group members as sub-systems (see Case Examples 5 and 12 in particular).

The issue of the therapist's 'selective perception' within a system is a most important one and often overlooked, I believe. Agazarian's point was well illustrated during an experiential workshop I attended in Zagreb, Yugoslavia, conducted by two American group analysts. The purpose of the workshop was to demonstrate their model of supervising trainees. The group was multi-cultural but predominantly made up of people with English as first language. One Yugoslav woman, whose English was very slight, was hesitant about speaking and when heavily challenged by the conductors pointed out her difficulty in understanding and communicating in English. This was interpreted by the conductors as 'her problem' i.e. using the lack of language not to participate fully. Yet, we were guests in her Serbo-Croatian speaking country! This is a somewhat crude example of the kind of imperialist attitude which can be transmitted by conductors who are not taking into account the context, or the system, within which they are operating. I mean by this the tendency to pathologise behaviour rather than try to understand it within particular social and cultural norms.

CAN INTERACTION BE ANTI-THERAPEUTIC?

This is a question which has to be addressed as, obviously, any treatment can be effective and successful or, on the other hand, have no effect or, worse, be damaging. Bloch and Crouch (1985: 82) draw our attention to Slavson's suggestion that interaction may not always be helpful, pointing out the potential for heightened discomfort in the interaction between members. An example would be of a very aggressive member 'terrorising' a very timid, nervous member, or of inaccurate and sadistic feedback. It is up to the therapist to manage the group dynamics appropriately so that their therapeutic effects will predominate and help members gain insight into their own and others' behaviour.

Scapegoating is another example of anti-therapeutic interaction (see Case Example No. 11) as is victimisation of any group member. Bion (1961) mentioned anti-therapeutic interactions in the form of so-called 'basic assumption' groups: that is, members resort to primitive strategies which deny reality and are irrational, even magical in quality. In a 'dependency' stage, a group may choose a leader (an alternative to the actual leader) who they fantasise will rescue them from their plight. In the process, the 'leader' is stuck in a position in which he cannot gain help for himself, and must even 'sacrifice' himself for the others. In another group, the members may persist in experiencing the conductor as all-powerful and hence themselves as powerless. (This is one of the dangers of certain kinds of 'theme-centred art therapy groups' pointed out by McNeilly.) Another basic assumption is 'pairing' where responsibility gets delegated to two members in the hope that out of their union will arise the solution to everyone's problems.

Bion's work is important as it emphasises the 'group-as-a-whole' in relation to and containing the therapist. He identified factors, such as those mentioned above, which interfere with the therapeutic potential of a group. These have to be identified in order for the group to do its curative work.

Another anti-therapeutic element which could apply to any group is premature termination of members caused by external pressures, lack of understanding about the nature of the group, scapegoating and even being referred elsewhere by another clinician! Surprising as it may seem, this has been known to happen. The conductor's role in understanding, possibly predicting and feeding back to the group about these anti-therapeutic processes is clearly vital. (See Yalom, 1985: 190–1, who mentions such processes as 'taking turns' in speaking which can force members into premature self-disclosure or into extreme anxiety as their turn approaches, or to devoting the whole group to the first issue; collaborative collusion in avoiding certain issues, and so on.)

Having explored some of the theories and manifestations of interactive groups, I would now like to focus on those aspects which are held to be 'curative' and how the introduction of art materials and the making of images in an interactive group can add to or enhance the process of positive change. I shall also look at some of the problems involved in extending the model in this way, and at the particular responsibilities for the conductor of an interactive art therapy group.

NOTE

1 Theme-centred interactive workshops are fairly widely used – in London an organisation 'Will' has been active in promoting this model.

Chapter 3

Curative factors in groups

This chapter will first summarise what are usually considered to be the specific advantages or curative factors in interactive groups and ask the question: Why introduce art therapy into the group and what might be the advantages, and problems, of doing so?

INTRODUCTION

There are several features of psychotherapy groups in general which are considered by most workers in the field to have curative potential. In summary, these are:

1 Giving and sharing of information: this happens in the early stages of a newly formed group when members impart information about themselves and the therapist helps members to understand the task of the group, namely that the members should interact, share thoughts and feelings and give feedback to each other as honestly as possible.
2 Installation of hope: new members need to see that the group is worth joining and that others have benefited. Usually the other group members will 'initiate' a new member and point out positive changes that have happened to individuals and to the group. Members usually reassure a new person that the group is valuable and worthwhile (although on occasions a member who is angry with the conductor and with the group will deride the group in an attempt to form an anti-conductor sub-group, which will need to be picked up by the conductor or, preferably, other group members).
3 Patients help each other. It is difficult at first for patients to feel that they can be helped by other patients and a common fear is that they will be adversely affected by each other's neurosis, so they look to the leader to 'give the answers'. Gradually they find that they can be helpful to and helped by other patients and it is of course up to the therapist to encourage this to happen and not to collude with the fantasy that he or she is all-powerful.

4 Patients discover that others have the same problems, anxieties and fears. They are not alone with their problem. There may be someone in the group who has overcome this particular difficulty who can provide hope that it can be resolved or changed.

5 The small group acts as a reconstruction of the family – members can use each other to work out feelings about brothers, sisters, mothers, fathers, etc. One of the big advantages that groups have over individual therapy is the access to a network of relationships, thus the multiplicity of transferences which occur and can be examined. Medium and large groups have specific features and tend to echo the community or our larger social group.

6 Catharsis – when a member confesses to a state of mind which they had previously hidden, to desires and fantasies they had been deeply ashamed of, or relives a traumatic event in the group – usually brings great relief. It often leads to similar 'confessions' by other members and helps to bring the group members closer.

7 People can learn how they interact with others and have some feedback about this. They can practise different ways of relating within a safe structure. Of course the member must feel sure there is no question of 'retaliation' by another member outside the group, and this is why members are advised not to have social contacts outside as it could interfere with their freedom to interact in the group. Sometimes this is unavoidable and the therapist would then ask patients to bring material from interactions outside into the here-and-now of the group. In a training group, this material can be very useful to the students' overall learning about group interactive processes. 'Assessment' by the conductor and by peers is liable to be a major preoccupation in a training group, giving rise to members' questioning what information may safely be shared. Provided this is acknowledged right from the start, it can be useful material and not inhibit interaction.

8 Group cohesiveness. The group is valued by its members as a safe place where deepest feelings can be shared without fear or retribution and where confidences can be shared and trust established. The group could be said to take the place of the 'super-ego' and can act as support or reinforcer during the week and when new behaviour is being tried out. The group – and the conductor by modelling a non-judgemental attitude – may also modify the super-ego of patients who tend to treat themselves and others very harshly.

9 Interpersonal learning. The group provides an opportunity for the past to be re-played in the present with the opportunity for feedback and change. Old, unsuccessful and frustrating patterns of behaviour can be uncovered, examined and hopefully improved.

The overall aim of group therapy is, of course, for members to uncover their unconscious feelings and how these affect their lives in the here-and-now.

Only psychotherapy groups can perform this task effectively – other groups, such as activity groups, work therapy, social skills, do not have this primary task, although incidentally unconscious attitudes are often uncovered.

INTRODUCING ART THERAPY INTO PSYCHOTHERAPY GROUPS

There are several ways in which introducing art materials into a group alters the dynamics of the group.

Maclagan (1985: 7), writing of his experience of conducting art therapy groups in a therapeutic community where verbal groups were the 'norm' makes the following comment:

> Art therapy represents a potentially dangerous encounter with the irrational and the uncontainable. It also involves a shift of competence, from a verbal domain that is to some extent an instrument of rationalisation and control, to a non-verbal (or marginally verbal) area that is unfamiliar (I can't draw), of dubious value (It's just a picture), and potentially humiliating (It's all turned out wrong). Nonetheless, it does address itself with a paradoxical intentionality – to those very areas of experience (dream, fantasy, imagination) that are usually kept hidden behind veils of literal or anecdotal subject matter: indeed, the real struggle of Art Therapy is not so much with language as such, as with the concretising, proprietorial tendencies to which it gives most emphatic expression.

Let us look, then, at some of the advantages and problems involved in this 'potentially dangerous encounter with the irrational':

1 Most people, unless they have severe speech handicaps, are used to communicating in words and not in images. Our grasp of non-verbal communication is therefore less sophisticated than spoken language, so we have fewer established defence patterns. Although as children we may have drawn and painted freely, and this activity is vital to our overall development (see Matthews, 1989), we tend to give it up as adults. Coming into an interactive art therapy group may present adult patients with their first experience of using art materials for many years – or their first ever experience. Wadeson (1987: 143) comments that making art may give rise to 'performance fear' – not being good enough and, for this reason, group members may feel more at risk and need much trust in each other in order to share private, not easily controlled imagery. However, once having risked exposure of a vulnerable image, a member usually feels more trusting of the group and the whole group develops an atmosphere of trust (1987: 143).

2 The art materials give a means of expression additional to or alternative

to words; they can be used in an experimental way and here it is up to the therapist to provide the kind of materials that can be used flexibly and do not have too many connotations of the classroom or art academy (see Chapter 5). The patient can be encouraged to 'play' with the materials. Of course many people feel very inhibited to start with, but someone in the group is usually willing to start and this encourages the others. Patients are often very surprised by the work that they and the group produce when they had felt themselves to be 'not good' at art.

Conversely, art graduates often experience much difficulty and embarrassment about being in an art therapy group and will try to differentiate between their 'real' artwork (made 'outside') and that made in the group: i.e. that work over which they can exercise conscious control and that which is made spontaneously and as a result of the group process. As time goes on, the distance between the two sets of work often decreases and, ideally, they may become freer both in their artwork and in their interactions.

3 Image-making within a group is rather akin to 'free association' or 'dreaming onto paper'. It can lead to forgotten or repressed incidents being re-enacted in a very powerful and cathartic way. These incidents can be shared with the group and hopefully exorcised of their power (see Case Example No. 6).

4 The art objects are full of symbolic meaning, both to the individual who produced them and to the group. These meanings are not necessarily the same. As in verbal group therapy, the use of metaphor and symbol is very important. Wadeson points out that the message of the images is received visually by other group members and affects them, whether or not they can describe their reactions. Words are often inadequate to convey an entire experience, whereas images tap into aspects of being that are not necessarily able to be articulated verbally (Wadeson, 1987: 144).

5 The artwork also aids understanding of the here-and-now of the group. The group can reflect on all the images made by each individual from the perspective of how the image relates to the individual and also to the group as a whole. The therapist can draw attention to similarities among images and to specific issues – e.g. polarisation.

Wadeson (1987: 47) points out that the process of the group may become illuminated through images as well as words and additonally through reflection on the images. Individual feedback may be eloquently given as group members make pictures of one another. The development of the group as a whole may be seen in each member's view of the group at a particular time or an issue facing the group presented in art expression (see Case Example No. 5).

By reflecting and by observing content and affect respectively, a group's theme or mood may be revealed. Sometimes the artwork is so dramatically revealing that there is no need for a therapist to make a process comment (as in a verbal group). On the other hand, when group processes are not so evident, the art may serve as a useful reference point for the therapist's commentary.

6 The group's attitude towards the conductor at any particular time may be illustrated by several individuals quite concretely: e.g. hearts and flowers just before a break accompanied by scenes of destruction and despair (see Case Example No. 12).

7 The artwork is the focus for projection. Sometimes the use of certain materials, like finger-paint or clay, can cause very early feelings to emerge and the group members to regress accordingly. Members can identify with (or 'resonate' to) each other's work. It might not be possible or even necessary to talk about this work, but members might want to return to it at a later stage. Work is stored and can be brought out again and again, and perhaps changed or even destroyed. This process can continue for several weeks if necessary, or for as long as time is available (see Case Example No. 3).

8 The artwork is a focus for interaction. I have found that when people are unfamiliar with the art therapy process, they expect that the therapist will give interpretations of the artwork: what does it mean? Please diagnose my condition. These are early requests. Somehow, having the art object available invites these requests, even from sophisticated patients. The question is put back to the patient and the group – how did you feel about that? How did you feel when making it? What do other people think? What does it mean to the group? The therapist's task is to encourage interaction between members, and to make comments to the group as a whole – by identifying similar elements in people's paintings, by linking the themes of one week with those before, etc. It is entirely unhelpful for the therapist to collude with wishes to interpret the paintings (rather like reading tea-leaves) as this disempowers the group.

9 The practical nature of the group provides a structure which is for many people less threatening than a verbal group. They can, if they need, preoccupy themselves with the materials and feel less exposed than in a verbal group. They can, for the time being at least, say 'It's just a picture.' This is helpful to people who have the potential to benefit from a group but find the exposure to others too threatening to begin with and might be likely to leave.

10 Because using art materials always contains an element of play, the group can have a 'fun' aspect as well as being serious. When adults can let themselves go enough, or regress sufficiently, to enjoy play, it can quickly help them to get in touch with patterns of behaviour which are causing problems. For example, the person who was never allowed to play at home, or got left out of games with other children. The one who always had to dominate, or the one who could never make themselves

heard. The shared processes of making, as in a group painting, quickly reveal family patterns, and each individual will respond according to their experience in the family (see Case Example No. 4).

11 The imagery left behind after each session is of great value to the therapist when reflecting on the process. It is a container for so much that has gone on, a reminder of each individual and of the process of the group. However, knowing what to do with the imagery – i.e. where to store it safely, etc., gives an additional responsibility to the conductor (see Chapter 5).

What to do with the imagery – and the room – when the group has finally ended gives further useful material for interaction (see Case Example No. 13).

12 The group process may be intensified through the introduction of art materials. A feature of using art therapy as part of a group process is that processes may develop very quickly, and are made visible, more tangible and available for working on. But it is precisely because of the speed and intensity provoked by image-making in an interactive group, that the conductor must be firmly in control, through their own training, and able to slow the process down if it seems that too much material is being produced without adequate processing. The group may be trying to avoid experiencing the emotion of a particularly difficult or painful event (e.g. a long-standing member leaving, the Christmas break approaching, etc.) by producing vast amounts of imagery which is left in undigested piles. At such times, the conductor's role may feel similar to that of a conductor in a psychodrama group (see Holmes, 1991: 7–13 for a useful introduction to classical psychodrama).

13 The value of creative activity. This element of the group process should not be overlooked. For many people, engaging in the art-making process is in itself challenging, rewarding and stimulates learning. Quite often greater flexibility in using materials goes hand in hand with a willingness to experiment with relationships in the group. Many of the objects and paintings produced in art therapy groups are remarkable for their originality. Even people who consider themselves 'clumsy' and 'uncreative' can, through the group process, open themselves up to the possibilities of the art materials.

In summary, the above curative factors are contained within a group interactive model, in which the making of images facilitates interaction among members and the therapist and stimulates the creativity of participants. The model also involves awareness of the group as a 'system' and willingness to use the social and cultural context of the group and its images as material for the group. As in verbal group therapy, the conductor avoids focussing on the individual, or on the overt 'content' of the session, but encourages the members to interact, being aware of the symbolic, metaphoric messages arising both from the images and the relationships among the members themselves.

Having suggested ways in which the group interactive process can be enhanced or changed by the introduction of image-making, in the following chapter I shall explore some of the specific responsibilities involved in conducting an interactive art therapy group.

Chapter 4

Conducting an interactive art therapy group

The extent to which a conductor believes that participants in a group are able to make their own choices, i.e. of themes or in structuring the group, is one of the main factors influencing their approach. In Chapter 1 we have seen how the discussion about theme-centred versus 'non-directive' groups dominated the art therapy literature on groups for some time. Personally I believe it is possible to work with themes which arise in both the artwork and the verbal interaction at the same time as drawing on insights from group analytic and interactive models. I think it would be very difficult, though, for the conductor constantly to provide emotive themes (i.e. draw your family) and work with transference or even with group-as-a-whole issues in any meaningful way. This would seem to limit the potential of the group to arrive at its own themes, or 'resonances' in its own time. It is possible, as I hope to show later, in a short-term training group for example, for the conductor to introduce open-ended projects designed to promote interaction such as 'introduce yourself visually to the group' which leaves members plenty of scope to be as open or closed as they feel able at that time. The conductor can also encourage expression of feeling around doing this task at the request of the conductor. In the early stages of a group, this constitutes 'information sharing' visually and verbally, and the conductor opens up the possibility of members being able to react freely to him or herself. The group interactive art therapist accepts that group members are at liberty to ignore any suggestion he or she makes in favour of their own resolutions.

Aveline and Dryden have succinctly described the features of an interpersonal or interactive group:

> The philosophical underpinning in existentialism in the interpersonal group leads to a distinct emphasis on members taking responsibility for their actions, being authentic and exercising their freedom of choice, a feature of practice of gestalt group therapy too. This serious note is balanced by an emphasis on humour, an element shared with psy-

chodrama and gestalt, which in turn, stresses the vitalizing force of creativity and spontaneity.

(1988: 144)

On a light note, they mention a categorisation scheme developed by a literary critic, Northrop Frye in the 1950s and 1960s, which was later applied by Schafer to psychoanalysis in a book on language (Schafer, 1976) and subsequently by Messer (1986) to psychoanalytic therapy and behaviour therapy. Life's possibilities are divided into four themes: the romantic, ironic, tragic and comic visions. In applying these thematic structures to small group therapies, Aveline and Dryden see the analytic group therapies as predominantly tragic, with their emphasis on underlying unconscious conflicts which have to be faced; and romantic in their belief that full human potential can be realised. The conductor is the spokesman for the ironic vision because he or she helps the group look below the surface. The interpersonal approach is also tragic and romantic but leavened by the comic:

> In its humanism, the approach is hopeful about the individual and what that person may achieve with the help of the group, but its existential heritage confers a tragic realisation of the inevitability of death and unfulfilled ambitions.

(Aveline and Dryden, 1988: 145)

The leaders of analytic and interpersonal groups have much in common – i.e. they do not actually lead (as, say, in gestalt or psychodrama groups) but the analytic leader interprets the communications of the group and the social matrix, remaining in the background as much as possible and helping the group take responsibility for itself: 'The role is austere and highly professional; it is not to give comfort or be real – hopefully members will give this to each other' (Aveline and Dryden, 1988: 148). (By 'real' I take the authors to mean revealing the true feelings that the conductor may have in the group.)

Whereas:

> the interpersonal leader is seen as a facilitator of interpersonal transactions and as a fellow-traveller in the journey of life; taking an increasingly background role, he attends to the language, both verbal and physical, that is used in the group and its meaning.

(Aveline and Dryden, 1988: 148)

Aveline and Dryden also discuss personality characteristics of effective leaders of the various small group approaches: the analytic leader, they say, demonstrates his 'analytic love of truth even when unpalatable' and the interpersonal and gestalt leader 'acts as a model of good membership: he tries to be open, shows willingness to change, takes risks and is relatively undefended. . .' (1988: 149).

According to Ratigan and Aveline (1988: 54):

The leader as a facilitator of interpersonal transactions is neither passive nor claims the centre stage but will be both observer and reflector of what is going on in the group. The latter role obviously has echoes of the psychoanalytic perspective. The leader also models helpful group behaviour to the members and in this perspective is linked with social learning theory (Bandura, 1977).

Thompson and Khan (1988: 77–8) point out that the conductor is as subject to the influence of the group culture as the members (and indeed helps to create it) but he or she must be sufficiently detached from it to be aware of what is going on and be able to intervene when necessary – for example, to prevent scapegoating, as in Case Example No. 11). The conductor needs to recognise group processes and the way in which they and other members are contributing, for every intervention that a group psychotherapist makes, or does not make, is significant. It is through the attitude and behaviour of the conductor that a group can learn tolerance and a permissive and accepting attitude (and conversely, of course, an authoritarian and punitive attitude). Through their own experience in therapy, the group leader should have learned how to tolerate distressing experiences and to enable the group to do the same.

To sum up, the major functions of the group conductor are to:

1 establish and sustain the group's boundaries (selection and preparation of members, organising of the group room, receiving apologies, etc.);
2 model and maintain a therapeutic group culture; i.e. one in which tolerance and a permissive, accepting attitude prevails;
3 provide an understanding of the events of the session and encourage group members to do the same;
4 note and remind members of their progress and change since being in the group;
5 encourage members to take responsibility for their actions;
6 predict (and possibly prevent) undesirable developments, such as scapegoating, victimisation, acting out, premature termination of member, misleading feedback being given;
7 involve silent members – preferably by pointing out how the group process has enabled a member to remain 'the silent one';
8 increase cohesiveness (by drawing attention to similarities between members in the group);
9 provide hope for members (it helps members to realise that the group is an orderly process and that the leader has some coherent sense of the group's long-term development).

The leader also has to be aware of the 'culture' of the group and here Thompson and Khan draw a parallel between the group and the nation state. They point out that disruptive elements in the state can be dealt with either by tolerance of rebellious or subversive activity in the case of a confident state or by repression, censorship and insistence on conformity in the case of a divided or threatened state. Groups may also develop a culture which discourages non-conformity and makes certain subjects 'taboo' areas or only to be discussed at certain times (e.g. when the leader is absent).

Having looked at some of the general features of a conductor's role, let us now turn to the conductor of an art therapy group and see what some art therapists have said about this.

Wadeson (1980), writing as an art therapist who often conducts groups, believes that the sort of leader one chooses to be depends on such factors as type of client population, size of group, treatment goals, length of treatment, setting, structure of sessions and personal style.

In common with verbal group conductors, Wadeson sees part of her role as modelling behaviour for the group – demonstrating dedication, acceptance, respect for others and empathy. She is aware of and pays close attention to power issues involved in conducting (1980: 240). As with verbal groups, she has a management role in determining the length of sessions, admission of members, fees, etc. She pays attention to time boundaries – she arrives on time and encourages others to do the same. She maintains the ending time of the group. She tries not to be judgemental and does her best to create a climate in which everyone's insights and observations are valuable.

Writing about her experiences in a day hospital run on therapeutic community lines in the 1970s, the late Patricia Nowell Hall saw art therapy groups as providing 'a necessary balance to the somewhat heavy emphasis on verbal, interpretive and analytic groups' (Nowell Hall, 1987: 157–87). She conducted two art therapy groups each week, one open to everyone and the other an intensive group for six to eight people with a commitment for a fixed length of time. She structured the art therapy groups in three stages: first, people would come together for a short general discussion and have the chance to express how they felt at that time; second, they would find a space and paint, usually working alone for about an hour; third, they would come together as a group, with a turn for each person to show and talk about their paintings if they wished. Sometimes exercises were suggested – generally designed to facilitate self-exploration rather than prescribe areas to explore. Usually the sessions were 'open' and relatively 'non-directive'. Nowell Hall kept the paintings in folders and encouraged group members to look at them again regularly in the following months, individually and in series.

She said of her role as conductor:

As the art therapist in the groups, I aspired, as Champernowne (1969) said 'to provide the protective conditions to let things happen', and to enable the ideal that Carl Rogers (1957: 95–103) claims as 'the necessary therapeutic climate'. This would be one that allows both psychological safety and freedom – through unconditional positive regard, warmth, genuineness and accurate empathy, thereby maximising the chance of openness to play, to experiment, and to change and for constructive creativity and growth to emerge.

(Nowell Hall, 1987: 159)

She went on to say that she saw the role of the therapist as being like a 'psychic midwife' helping to bring things to birth, or a 'gardener', enriching the ground and helping the seeds to grow. In this respect, she echoes the attitudes of the advocates of 'child art' such as Franz Cizek, Wilhelm Viola, Marion Richardson, who believed that, given the right conditions – space, non-judgemental attitude, art materials – the inherent creativity of the child would emerge. (See Waller, 1991: 16–24 for further information on the 'child art' movement.)

It goes without saying that the art therapist conductor should be thoroughly at home with a wide range of art materials, enjoy the process of visual creativity and be open and flexible in his or her approach to making images. If the conductor does not themselves have an extensive background in visual art, then they should co-conduct with someone who does. It is unlikely that the important element of enhanced creativity will be present in a group if the conductor is entirely inexperienced in the use of materials or has rigid preconceptions about art.

The conductor of an interactive art therapy group has the responsibility of providing and maintaining a suitable room which is large enough for participating in art-making. This room will need suitable furniture for the purpose and the conductor needs to provide a stock of basic art-making materials. The conductor has to ensure that work can be safely stored after each session and that the artwork is named and dated. He or she also has to see that health and safety precautions are upheld – e.g. firing kilns, seeing that pottery glazes, knives and other instruments are properly used (see Chapter 5 for discussion of these important issues).

The issue of using time within the session for talking and/or making images is also one which exercises the leader of an art therapy group. In a verbal group, members have a clear task – to communicate through words, usually sitting in a circle. Generally they speak one at a time and though they may interrupt each other, several people are not normally trying to communicate at once. In an art therapy group, the conductor has to decide whether to influence the structure of the group – i.e. by suggesting how long to paint for and to talk for, or letting the group make this decision. Some members may be painting, others talking, some working individually, others sharing a piece of paper. There are many interactions for the leader to be aware of at once.

McNeilly (1990), while a student at the Institute of Group Analysis, presented a seminar to his peer group on the adaptation of group analysis to his own work as an art therapist. Although he has evolved a group-analytic art therapy approach, his findings are, I believe, equally applicable to an interactive approach. McNeilly reported the following observations made by the student group:

> It was more demanding for the group-analytic art therapist to sit watching and remain alert for the first forty-five to sixty minutes (the image-making period) while many simultaneous expressions occur. Perhaps it was at this seminar that I began to develop my view that this part of the art therapy group is like 'classical free association', whereas in conventional group analysis 'group associations' occur throughout the session.
>
> (1990: 217)

McNeilly points out that at the beginning of his groups, members create their own images concurrently. If people were all speaking at once in group analysis this would be chaotic or nonsensical. Therefore the verbal group analyst works through consecutive verbal inputs. He found that his colleagues were surprised that:

> so much resonance and cohesion could be reached when people had the freedom to create their separate imagery, to emerge in the verbal section united or fighting, like the best of groups. There was a prior view that the opposite would occur – that people would become more isolated from one another.
>
> (McNeilly, 1990: 217–18)

McNeilly, like Nowell Hall, does structure the use of time of his groups, that is, he prescribes a certain time for image-making and a time for talking. Nowell Hall described how this process worked in her groups:

> The art therapy session offered a balance of privacy and sharing: first to withdraw, reflect and explore, through the art materials, alone, intrapsychically and silently; and then to 'come out' and come together with others for showing and talking – each with his own individual and unique creation to show and/or talk about. In this way the private world of painting became linked to the public world of language, and with an intermediate stage of being able to communicate with and confront oneself first, before sharing with others. This was commented on as very important, especially in a milieu that was in a sense based on a more extroverted and interpersonal group therapy culture.
>
> In this way the art therapy activity offered an opportunity to begin to develop the vital capacity to be separate and alone (all-one) in order to be healthily together with other people.
>
> (Nowell Hall, 1987: 165–6)

One can see from these quotes how Nowell Hall's basic Jungian and Rogerian philosophy influences the way she both perceives the function of this group, how she structures it and her role within it. The interaction in this art therapy group is mainly between herself as conductor and the individual members, and the members and their artwork. This group might well have served an important function in enabling patients who would otherwise have found the verbal groups too confrontative to make use of them subsequently if they so wished.

Sally Skaife has explored the issue of structuring the group's time for art-making and for talking in her article 'Self-determination in group analytic art therapy' (1990) in which she describes an art psychotherapy group which attempts to combine two types of therapeutic practice, free-floating verbal interaction and individual involvement in visual self-expression, allowing the group to decide when and how they change activity. Skaife says:

> The art activity adds a new dimension to the 'work material' of the analytic group, allowing as it does for feelings to be expressed in an alternative way and metaphorical and symbolic language to stay on in the group in a concrete form. As well as this, feelings that are not easily expressed in words can be played with in their symbolic form, for instance, colour and shape, and thus worked on in a way that can make them more accessible to language and thus to consciousness. As in other art therapy settings, group members are encouraged to use the art materials to express themselves freely; this work is then looked at as both belonging to the history of the individual and as an expression of the dynamic of the group.
>
> (1990: 237)

Skaife questions the conductor structuring the group time. She considers that if she decides how long the group should paint for and talk for, there is a danger of her being too controlling or interfering with the transference; that she may interrupt the group process and curtail important interactive therapeutic work. The method she tends to use is to leave the group to decide on when and how they should paint, the processes that influence these decisions then being subject to analysis in the same way as other aspects of group life.

Skaife has found that one positive outcome of this approach is that members can reflect on their own contribution to decision-making and thus develop greater understanding of their own ways of negotiating social relations. In addition, Skaife points out, issues particular to 'creative activity', such as the ability to 'let go', tolerate chaos and so on, emerge frequently for discussion as members are responsible for their own actions.

Her article contains a case study vignette of a group in which there was pressure for her to structure the time. She makes the important point:

In group therapy individuals repeatedly lose themselves in the group identity and then find themselves as unique individuals. Painting, however, is essentially an individual activity. When the group stop talking and begin to paint energy becomes focused away from others and on to the self (though group painting alters this to some extent). By allowing the group to decide how and when they should change activity one is bringing into focus issues such as the use of time, being alone and being part of a group. Letting go of the group to go and paint was likened by E. to entering chaos.

(1990: 243)

The art-making process, then, adds a complex other dimension to group psychotherapy, whether group analytic or group interactive or a combination of both.

I mentioned in Chapter 3 that, at certain times in the group, i.e. when the group is producing vast quantities of images and showing no signs of wanting to 'digest' these or reflect upon them, the conductor's role may resemble that of a psychodrama conductor. There is a high degree of 'drama' in an interactive art therapy group (see Case Examples 6, 7, 8, 11 and 12 in particular) and the conductor may need to be particularly vigilant in reinforcing boundaries and encouraging members to move into a different mode of enactment, to slow the process down. Personally, I would recommend participating in several sessions of psychodrama for any conductor of interactive art therapy groups, so that they may feel more secure about that aspect of their role which is concerned with keeping the group members 'in role'. As Case Example No. 11 shows, images are sometimes so powerful that they overwhelm both the maker and the group and the symbolic, or 'as if' qualities are likely to be lost.

At such times, I would tend to think that the conductor of an interactive art therapy group, requires, like Aveline and Dryden's psychodrama group conductor: 'an uncommon blend of extroversion and sensitivity, as well as energy and the ability to think on one's feet and to tolerate the scrutiny of the group in the prominent role of director' (1988: 149).

The question of what to do with the productions after the session has ended is one which always faces an art therapist conductor and is particular to their role. Art therapists normally have a ground rule that images are left in the room, i.e. they are not taken away by the members, nor are they interfered with between group sessions. In Case Example No. 11 I shall describe how devastating a violation of this rule can be for a group. Members leave their 'symbolic selves' in the safe-keeping of the therapist. The therapist has the problem of how to store the images. This is particularly difficult if space is very limited or if the room is to be used soon after by others. Indeed, the scope of image-making itself may be limited by such reality factors: it is a problem if the group create a structure which needs to be left up if others are going to use the space. Spontaneity in the process usually has to be curtailed by these practical considerations and this is a serious limitation in the potential of the interactive approach. It is, however, one which is difficult to solve, given that there are usually space problems in most institutions. The ideal would be a room which was used by one group, perhaps over a limited period, and in which the group could create its own environment.

Possibly the fact that space has to be shared and is usually limited contributes to most art therapists talking about drawing and painting in groups, as opposed to sculpting or building environments. I believe it is an important issue to be addressed. Working on small sheets of sugar paper with felt-tipped pens in someone's office may certainly be of use but is bound, in my view, to limit the therapeutic potential of the group. Using tables in the dining room prior to lunch being served is also inhibiting and although one can say that it is useful to work with limitations of reality and to see how group members circumvent them, it is unreasonable to see this as anything but part of the potentially more vital and energy-releasing process which could develop with appropriate resources. I speak from experience here: as we shall see from some of the case examples in this book, I have conducted interactive art therapy groups in a variety of spaces, some ideally suited to my purpose, others almost impossible. I have therefore learned 'the hard way' and will be sure to ask for minimal working space and conditions before undertaking to run a group.

One of the important functions particular to an art therapist conductor then, is the practical one of ensuring that art materials are available and a suitable space in which to use them can be provided. That this task is not always straightforward will be clear from the examples in the next chapter.

Chapter 5

Practical matters
Materials and rooms

ART MATERIALS

In Britain, trainee art therapists are usually art graduates. In any case, they have extensive practical experience of using art materials and most people have had art education in their school curriculum. This is by no means the case elsewhere. For many years now I have been conducting art therapy groups in various institutions in eastern and western Europe. These institutions have actively sought to introduce art therapy into their training or treatment programmes and the following observations are offered as a result of the experience gained from this work.

In parts of Europe, art education is not in the school curriculum and trainees who undertake art therapy are often psychiatrists, psychologists and nurses who have little or even no practical experience of art. This is not seen as a problem, because art therapy is part of a medical tradition, and therapists are not artists. The concept of 'lay', i.e. non-medical, psychother-apists is not always accepted. It is possible that as a result of the European Community and greater movement between eastern and western Europe, the training and background of art therapists will become more 'harmo-nised'. Just now, though, we have to accept that there are differences in basic education and that trainees approach art therapy with very varied backgrounds.

It is a strongly held view in Britain and in the USA that art therapists should either have been art trained or have ability in and commitment to the practice of a visual art. This gives confidence in the image-making process, an understanding of the symbolic language of art and its power to communicate. It gives the therapist greater freedom to respond to a patient's images, and I have mentioned the importance of this in Chapter 4. Without such 'visual confidence' there is a tendency for a 'reductive' attitude to be taken to the image: that is, a search for equivalence in words and for a judgemental approach to underlie an observation: 'This is not art.'

That is not to say that all artists are immune from these attitudes nor that all non-artists will have such a reaction to an image. It is rather that the long, often lonely road that the art student travels in their struggle with drawing, painting, sculpting or whatever visual art form they have chosen, can, perhaps, be compared to a personal analysis. The unknown has to be faced: the blank sheet of paper or the canvas or the concept has to be grappled with; ideas are difficult to put into forms. The artist is faced with themselves, their attitudes and assumptions, and has to draw on their own resources. There is also the development of art within a social context to be studied – movements such as Surrealism, Pop Art, Abstract Expressionism, Happenings, Conceptual Art and so on. Images have a social and cultural context; colour has different symbolic meanings according to its cultural context; very young children are liable to use materials in a different way from the elderly – and so on. I believe, from experience, that the artist is less likely to 'pathologise' images – that is, search for signs of 'mental illness' – but to relate the image to the person who made it and seek their response. This is hardly possible if the art therapist has no experience of image-making themselves. As artists, we may have been deeply influenced by certain 'schools' of art – perhaps the one that was most prevalent when we were at art school; we may have biases and subtly encourage patients to paint, make pottery and so on when we need to be encouraging them to find their own most appropriate medium. We have to try and be aware of this and it isn't always easy. It is also not easy for an artist to be a participant in an art therapy group.

David Maclagan makes a further pertinent point in his discussion of the 'mythology of art therapy':

> The mythology of Art Therapy is, like so many other myths, a tactical exaggeration; due, perhaps to its need to defend itself against being used as an accomplice of psychiatric diagnosis. Amongst patients the fear is still there, that therapeutic painting or drawing is a kind of imaginary ambush, in which their relaxation will be taken analytical advantage of: this fear is all the more easily aroused in Art Therapy since, unlike the transitory verbal material of other groups, pictures are 'fixed' and thus far more exposed to scrutiny.
>
> (1985: 7)

How can participants express themselves visually, though, when they have no idea of the potential of materials and when their idea of Art is painting by Rembrandt or Leonardo da Vinci or other 'old masters'? This, in countries so rich in traditional art forms, which have been undervalued by reason of association with 'the past', which often means 'the village'. Or when Art may mean classical music, poetry, architecture or picture restoration . . . the use of the term 'art therapy' has uncovered many different understandings of the meaning of the word 'Art'.

This problem became clear when I first worked with a group of psychiatrists in Bulgaria. Only two people in the group had any experience of visual art whatsoever and that was a little painting at school. The reasons for their choosing to enter art therapy are complex and have been described elsewhere (see Waller, 1983/84, 1990). They were enthusiastic, all had an interest in 'Art' but had no idea about art materials, which, for art therapy trainees, is unthinkable in the UK.

There is an assumption in art therapy – perhaps also part of the mythology described by Maclagan – that the greater the range of choice in materials available the greater the range of expression and communication available to the patient. In an interactive group, such flexibility of expression, using art media, is a big plus.

There is also an assumption that each material has its own character and patients will respond to some materials rather than others at different times. If we accept these assumptions, then we must accept the responsibility of providing as wide a range of materials as is feasible. However, too great a range of unfamiliar materials can cause inhibition.

As a result of working in countries where art materials are very hard to come by and expensive, I have explored the concept of 'art materials' in some depth. I ask myself 'What are art materials? What assumptions have I been making?' In fact, reading *Studio International* recently, I wondered if materials were even necessary to make art, such was the emphasis on words! I asked for people's views about art materials in the first meetings of the Bulgarian training group. People replied: 'Oil paint, canvas, paper, watercolours, sable brushes. This is what art-making is about.' I asked, 'Is it possible to get hold of these materials, then?' They replied, 'No, not unless you are a member of the artists' union or a student in the art academy.' I asked, 'How are we going to work this week because we have no canvas, oil paint, etc.?' Some people suggested paper and pencil, readily available. Others, watercolour blocks, which could be bought in toy shops. I suggested we would need an immense number of these blocks to do work of any size. One doctor said, 'But we always give children little pieces of paper because we don't have room to put up large paintings.'

From this interaction there were many important issues raised: first, the concept of real art being done on canvas with oil paints or with watercolour. Second, you could not buy these materials unless registered as a professional or trainee artist, or unless you had a contact in the network. They were also extremely expensive. Third, most Bulgarians live and work in cramped public and private spaces. Literally, there is not room for hanging up large works in most institutions, flats or houses. Fourth, being an artist is seen as a highly professional activity, like being a lawyer. It is only recently that art has been included in the high school curriculum and then it tends to be art history or teaching about architecture or similar. Practical art classes have traditionally taken place in out-of-school centres, and children who showed talent were directed towards the art 'gymnasium' at 14-plus. Although the population in general are very well informed about art and flock to see exhibitions, very few people have ever participated in art-making themselves.

In discussing these issues with participants and members of staff in the Medical Academy, we came to the conclusion that *media workshops* needed to be provided as part of the training. They are, in fact, provided within British art therapy training courses, but are more often used for extending one's range of skills. For example, learning about pottery or printmaking, attending a life-drawing class, making sculpture and so on. These media workshops would need to start at the beginning, looking at the nature of materials, fundamentals of mark-making and so on.

The media workshops have been an integral part of all the training courses I have conducted abroad and have been run by Dan Lumley, an artist and art teacher with much experience of art therapy. They are clearly set up to focus on materials and are not therapy groups although sometimes participants will try to turn Dan into a therapist! The introduction of these groups into training courses has been enormously beneficial according to the feedback from participants. We have observed a 'freeing up' in the practical work. After all, if you have absolutely no idea what to do with any particular material it is hard to make it work for you! It is too easy to say that experimentation is part of the process. That is true, but I firmly believe that it's possible to be more creative and experimental if starting from a secure, if modest, base. This has led me to consider whether having media workshops for patients in hospital, alongside art therapy sessions, would be a good idea. The movement 'Artists in Hospitals' (see the Attenborough Report, 1985) has led to many artists wanting to use their skills with groups of patients and others who don't usually have access to the arts. Co-operation between artists and art therapists may provide a most valuable additional resource for patients. It would also leave the art therapist freer to concentrate on their role as group conductor, knowing that the patients had a basic knowledge at least of how to use materials. It is a thought that needs more exploration in practice.

Many different ways of working with materials can be demonstrated through the media workshops, and assumptions about art can be questioned. The aim is to provide participants with a choice about how they use the material. Different perspectives on the image from various art historical and cultural standpoints may be presented. At the end of the workshops, we do not expect the participants to have absorbed all that has been presented and in no sense are these workshops designed to be equivalent to a full art training. But we hope that the participants will be in a state we can call 'fertile disorientation' which may prepare them for the group art therapy sessions and stimulate them to engage more deeply in art practice in the future.

Being educated in and conducting groups in Britain, where all manner of materials are easily available, it is easy to forget that this is not the case in some other countries. The definition of 'art' is so broad as to include all manner of images, constructions, landscapes – and it was a Bulgarian artist, Christo, who wrapped buildings, bridges, cliffs, in plastic and called it Art!

The tableaux and assemblages of Edward Kienholz and Bruce Conner, and the Magic Realism of Peter Blume are art, as are the brillo pads of Andy Warhol, the metal constructions of Anthony Caro, the wooden sculptures of Louise Nevelson. 'Happenings' are art, taking a walk in the country or planting daffodils is also art. Visual art can encompass a high degree of dramatic interaction. The collection 'Art Brut', brought together by the artist Jean Dubuffet and now housed in Lausanne, reveals an incredible range of ideas and imagery. Some of this work was produced by people who happened to be in psychiatric hospital; others worked away on their own and were considered to be 'eccentric': hence the term 'Outsider Art'. Sometimes I feel that as art therapists we can get stuck with paint and paper not only because we are usually short of space but because we may be a little trapped in the conventions of the traditional 'studio' and the convention of 'art as expression', when it refers to art therapy.

However, because it seems that we do need to have some materials to use in making images in art therapy, in Case Example No. 1, I will return to more 'down to earth' problems of finding them in places where there are no convenient art materials shops.

ROOMS

With the exception of those lucky people who have access to varying sizes of studio space in hospitals, art therapists have always had difficulty in finding suitable places to work. They have found themselves in disused laundries, washrooms, store-rooms, corridors. This problem is highlighted following moves into 'the community' as a result of the closure of large psychiatric hospitals. Many fine spaces have been lost and adequate substitutes often not found in day care centres (see Wood, 1992). When running verbal small groups, it is possible to use a moderately large office, complete with chairs and carpet, but art therapy can be messy, people need to move around and have access to water. Sometimes art therapy groups cannot take place because there is no suitable room. This seems a great pity but even purpose-built day centres usually don't take the needs of art therapy into account. Elegant, hygienic kitchens, neatly carpeted small-group rooms, dining rooms with pine furniture, but no pottery or empty room with tiled floor and a sink! Even when resourceful art therapists put down plastic sheeting and carry buckets of water back and forth, there is still the problem of what to do with the work after the group.

This is where it is important to have a place to store what might be quite large objects. When two or more art therapy groups are using the same space at different times, they are likely to have a territorial competition by producing large objects that are difficult to move, or which have to be left in the room because the paint is very wet, the clay is wet, the objects are fixed to the walls and so on. This is all useful material for the process (looking at the system in which the group takes place), although it does give the art therapist conductor certain problems, especially if a colleague is to use the room later! It is one reason why working in unsuitable spaces in hospitals is frustrating.

For example, in one hospital, the only possible space for a trainee to hold an interactive art therapy group was the dining room. The trainee brought the problem to supervision and the group explored whether this was, in fact, the only space and if so, if it was possible to run a group there. There was the possibility of interruptions, of patients associating the space with eating, of having to clear everything up and scrub the formica tables before lunch. Work could not be left on the tables, which limited the range of materials to be used. The trainee decided to accept the limitations, paying particular attention to ensuring that there would be no interruptions during the group. She provided only 'dry' materials with the exception of watercolour paints; these included felt tips, old magazines, fabric, different coloured paper, glue, crayons, charcoal. She considered self-hardening clay, but decided against it. She had a 'junk' box, with odds and ends assembled from the hospital store.

Her patients were elderly people whose mobility was limited. They felt secure with the 'dry' materials and were able to work in these conditions. It was still difficult, though, as despite attempts to make the space private for the duration of the group, several people came in and out and clearly it was not very hygienic to use an eating place for artwork. The elderly people could not experiment with unfamiliar materials. All signs of the group had to be removed each time, so an important element of the process was lost.

Art therapists are, however, able to make use of spaces which other staff might not want: for example, huts. At Goldsmiths' College, the Art Psychotherapy Unit has the use of three somewhat battered huts, put up as temporary accommodation several years ago. There is plenty of light, they have plain white walls and wooden or linoleum floors. Large and ancient square sinks have been installed, as have heaters and plan-chests for storing drawings and paintings. Folding tables and stools can be erected as the group members wish, or be propped up against the walls. There is room for storing largish objects at each end of the hut. It does not matter if paint is spilt: it can easily be mopped up or scraped up later. As the huts are only used by art therapy trainees, there is a respect for other groups' work (despite the territorialism referred to above).

Maintenance of the rooms is important as health and safety laws must be conformed with. Art materials can be dangerous: for example, clay and glaze dust can be inhaled; and although all glazes used for teaching purposes are lead free, they could be dangerous if accidentally swallowed. Sharp knives and scissors are potentially lethal weapons and if working with patients who have a history of violence, much care must be taken. Patients with HIV or Aids may cut themselves and in this case, it is imperative that full precautions are taken to avoid contamination. Patients who are mentally handicapped may not understand that paint is not edible.

If using a kiln, this must be in a separate room or guarded by a special lockable kiln guard. Great care must be taken when glazing and firing pottery.

All this – as well as conducting the group and understanding the processes of individuals and group-as-a-whole – is the responsibility of the art therapist conductor.

I have found it essential to ask what space is available, before agreeing to conduct any interactive art therapy group. In the past I have accepted statements like 'There's a really large room' without checking exactly what size is large. I have naively asked: 'Is it suitable for art therapy, does it have water in it?' and been assured that it is, and that there is water. On arrival I have discovered a well-carpeted seminar room, complete with smart chairs and tables, large enough to *seat* sixteen people who will not move around and with a small wash-basin and tap in the corner! In the same building was a magnificent attic, being used as a store-room, complete with terrace and hose-pipe point, with a lino floor, next door to toilets and wash-basins! Tactful negotiations resulted in this attic being given over to the art therapy group for a whole week and the community used it whenever they had an art therapy group subsequently.

During an interactive art therapy group, I feel it is very important that people can move around freely, be active with the materials and each other if they so wish. They can, of course, sit quietly in one space if that is appropriate at the time. I've realised that the image people often have of art therapy groups is of a class sitting at desks – because this is what art was like at school! It was at my school – we used a hall several minutes walk away, in which there were desks and chairs. We had an 'art cupboard' and painted still-lifes and themes. This school did not rate art very highly and I know of schools with magnificent suites of studios. But I think that many people's only experience of art was like mine at school, so it isn't surprising that 'art therapy' confuses.

All the examples given in this chapter point clearly to the fact that art therapy is a new discipline and to the strangeness of having art activities in places designed for care and treatment of patients. It was not such a problem in the old psychiatric hospitals with their rambling wards and huge spaces, and sometimes old craft rooms which had been converted to art therapy studios. There is a very different atmosphere in a group which can move freely and use materials creatively – working on large or small pieces when needed and not having to worry about the curtains, than in a group which is restricted to felt tips and paper or instant-dry clay in an office in a day centre. I am in no way denigrating work which is done in these circumstances but have emphasised this point because it is one which other professionals, quite understandably, tend to overlook when planning treatment centres or inviting an art therapist to run a group workshop. It is up to the art therapist to make their needs quite clear.

The way that a group modify and use a space and the materials available does constitute useful content for the group to work on. As I have tried to show, though, there are minimal requirements without which it is unreasonable to expect that the process of group interactive art therapy will be effective.

Chapter 6

Using themes or projects within an interactive model

So far I have discussed groups in which themes tend to arise spontaneously out of discussion among group members. There are times, though, when I have decided to present the group with a theme, or perhaps project is a better description, right at the beginning. This is usually when conducting time-limited workshops in which the participants need to understand about the potentiality of art therapy for themselves. On these occasions I have obviously stepped away from the group analytic end of the interactive spectrum. On the other hand, having presented the group with the idea for the project, it is up to the individual members and the group how they interpret it and how they subsequently use the material.

I have used the following open-ended projects with trainee art therapists, other professionals wanting an introduction to the process of interactive art therapy, patient groups – mainly of functioning out-patients with problems such as drug and alcohol addiction, eating disorders, depression and phobias. I have found them useful ways either to begin or to continue a time-limited workshop. They can be developed by each group according to its preoccupations at the time and to the level of the participants' abilities. All the projects give ample opportunity for exploration of simple visual media – which in the case of non-art trained participants can be extremely useful for confidence building.

Self-boxes

This is a project which is useful to introduce at the beginning of a new group. It encourages members to focus on how they present themselves to the outside world and how they feel 'inside'. It requires them to reflect on how much (if at all) they hide or disguise their feelings (or 'real selves') in the interests of conforming to others' expectations (or expectations of their own). The project makes use of ordinary cardboard boxes as a starting-point and requires a range of easy-to-use materials. There is something quite reassuring about a cardboard box. There is nothing intrinsically precious about it. It can be obtained from any store or supermarket. This fact is quite

Figure 1 Example of a 'self-box'

important when working with people who are unused to group psychother-apy or have no experience with art materials. The time taken to make the box can vary according to time available for the group: in a one-off, boxes can be made very quickly and spontaneously, with little attention being paid to the details. Participants can say what they would have done had they had more time, etc. The important thing is that they respond quickly and are prepared to discuss, in general terms, how they felt about the project. In a one-off group (say two hours) there will not be adequate time to go into detail of each person's box but it begins the process of reflection which can be continued later by participants on their own. I tell the group that it is up to each person whether or not they close the box up, and if they do, it is up to them if they open it to show the group in the discussion period. This is a caution against premature self-revelation and gives timid or reserved members permission to have a private space for as long as they wish.

See Figures 1 and 2 for examples of self-boxes made by participants in an introductory art therapy workshop. Both these women chose to make both the inside and outside visible: in the 'house', the roof can be opened and one can peep through the open windows and doors.

There are several ways of continuing this project, depending on time and group membership: either I might suggest to the group that they make individual environments for their boxes, or that they choose others to work with and make a communal environment, or we select names out of a hat for

Figure 2 Example of a 'self-box'

random small groups; or that the group decide themselves what to do with the boxes.

For example, an ongoing women's group had made boxes, discussed them and they were still in the same place in the room the following week. When the group came in, someone said, 'We had better get these boxes out to make more space.' The group moved towards the boxes, ready to take them outside. I asked them to pause and reflect on why they were doing this. Someone said, 'We've finished with that project last week'. Another said, 'Well I don't feel very happy putting my box outside. I felt last week that I didn't really say much about it.' Another said, 'I felt we talked so much about them I am bored with it.' A fourth person suggested that they might have another look, from the viewpoint of a week later. There was much discussion among the eight members: to put outside or not. I suggested they consider the boxes as symbolic selves and try to find a way forward from there. They decided not to put the boxes outside but to store them in a recess in the room, where they could still be seen. Having stacked them up hurriedly and spontaneously, they then began to look at the resulting structure. One said, 'I am totally squashed by your box and in fact, I'm at the bottom of the pile!' This person replied, 'I can't move my box because P.'s will fall down . . . and so will J.'s.' Everyone looked to see where they had ended up in the pile of boxes and for the rest of the session, the group discussed this 'accidental grouping' and whether or not they were satisfied with it. They moved the boxes round, took the whole pile down and began to reassemble it, negotiating who wanted to be where. It was a valuable experience as they had thought carefully about their position in the group and if that related to their position outside – i.e. were they always feeling 'bottom of the pile', or alternatively, having to prop others up. They also thought about the culture which had developed in the group: tending to 'give up on' themselves rather than persevere and see a task through to the end.

(Other examples of the development of 'self-boxes' are given in Case Examples 4 and 11.)

Symbolic portraits

Often without realising it, we absorb a lot of information about each other through our visual and sensual experience. We take note of body language, colour of clothes, hair, facial expressions, smell and these impressions can be immediate and happen before we have spoken to a person. This is often known as a 'gut reaction'. If I am running a time-limited group or series of groups, I might ask participants to begin by making 'symbolic portraits', trying to catch their first impressions of either all the group or a few members visually, using whatever medium comes to hand. I might suggest using a colour or a shape or 'ready-made' images from magazines. I do not exclude myself, as conductor, from being 'portrayed' and it is surprising how often the 'symbolic portraits' include the conductor, or how the different 'portraits' contain elements of the conductor. The group may discuss them after making, or leave them till the end of the group to see if their first impressions have been modified as a result of getting to know other members, and the conductor, more intimately.

For example, during the first group of an introductory programme with medical staff who had no art experience, most chose to use felt-tipped pens although one or two selected paint. I had asked them to do the task as a way of thinking about themselves and each other at the beginning of the group and trying to record these important first sensations. I had not specified whether the group should make portraits of all members or just a few. It turned out that this was significant because there was one member who nobody had chosen! This was a most difficult and tense situation because the member felt, quite rightly, ignored and that there must be something wrong with her, and the group felt guilty. We discussed this at length. I felt a bit responsible for her distress (because I had presented the idea in the first place) although I did realise that there was something important for us all to learn. I suggested that maybe the group had linked the ignored member to myself – she was very quiet and slightly 'out' of the group, which resembled my role as conductor at that time. Perhaps there was something difficult to

Figure 3 Image of the conductor

deal with and although people had made pictures of me, there was the 'unknown' bit which they couldn't tackle. This intervention opened up the discussion to consider people's frank terror at the prospect of the week ahead, whereas previously they had denied any nervousness or anxiety. It pulled in the 'ignored' member as she could then share her extreme anxiety with the others: the powerful anxiety had radiated from her and other members had backed off, not wishing to acknowledge this in themselves.

See Figures 3 and 4 for examples of 'portraits'. Figure 3 is clearly meant to be the conductor and Figure 4 is a portrait of one prominent member of the group, which could stand for an image of the conductor, too.

Body images (or life-sized portraits)

This is a shorthand term for a fairly complex task. It requires preparation as large sheets of paper, suitable for making life-sized portraits are required and sufficient space for working on them and fixing them on the walls. The best paper to use seems to be brown parcel wrapping paper as this is strong, inexpensive and a useful width. Occasionally I have introduced this project in what seemed like an unsuitably small area and it has been exciting how

Figure 4 Image of a group member as a cat

the group have managed to negotiate the space. This in itself is valuable for interaction purposes.

The project is flexible and can be adapted to suit any client or training group (see Case Examples 6 and 8 and the case example in Chapter 8). Briefly, group members divide into pairs, either randomly through names out of a hat, or they choose. Usually people prefer names out of a hat as it avoids the problem of who to choose and who to reject, and I point this out when it happens.

There are then two possible ways of proceeding: either I suggest that each person makes a life-sized image of the other as they see them, or as they would like them to be. The outline can be drawn by each person lying on a large sheet of paper, and it is up to the artist, in each case, to say how they want their subject to lie (see Figures 5 and 6). This stage of the project usually produces much laughter and a little embarrassment as people have to get close to do the drawing. If anyone is really unhappy about the intimacy of the outlining, they can find a way round it by fixing the paper on the wall and standing up against it to be drawn. The next phase usually consists of reflection (see Figure 7) and sometimes verbal communication between the two before the painting begins.

Another way is for each person to tell the other how they would like to be

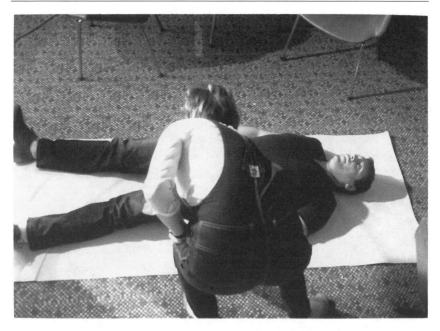

Figure 5 Preparing to make a life-sized portrait (body image)

Figure 6 Preparing to make life-sized portraits (body images)

Figure 7 Reflecting on each other

Figure 8 Fixing up a body image

painted. In this case, the artist must follow the subject. If the subject wants to be painted sitting down, or in an abstract way, then the artist has to follow suit (see Plates 1a and 1b, 2a and 2b for examples). Each person is alternatively the artist and the subject. This project illustrates how we project our fantasies onto others, or how we may use another to fulfil our fantasies of ourselves.

The next phase, once the paintings are finished, is to hang them on the walls around the room (Figure 8) so that a 'symbolic' group is formed. There are many uses for this group, according to how the actual group are feeling at that time. I usually suggest a period of time to discuss how the group members felt about the task and the results of the paintings. It is for most people quite a liberating experience to use large sheets of paper and plenty of paint, and gratifying to be the subject of someone else's careful attention. It can happen, though, that 'old scores' get settled by people who know each other outside the group, or one member choses to ignore the task and paint themselves rather than their partner (see Case Example No. 8).

All this will come up in the discussion. The next phase may be involving the whole group in looking at its symbolic self. I may suggest that members add or change certain aspects of a painting according to how they see that person. I might suggest that they negotiate with the painter first of all, before changing anything as obviously the images have become very important and meaningful to both partners. On one occasion I did not do this, and one group member who was containing much of the rebelliousness of the group and was, in fact, more daring than the others, went round adding very frank visual comments on all the paintings. This resulted in a furious discussion group in which he was in danger of being scapegoated as his behaviour had been perceived as provocative and even hostile. He was able to defend his position well and was not at all daunted and his frankness enabled the other members to interact more freely with each other. I stress the importance of periods of time for reflecting on the process as the images become laden with powerful projective material.

This can give rise to some negative as well as positive feelings and it is at thes: times that the process comes near to psychodrama in its realisation.

Again, there are many ways in which the project can continue. In a long-term group, the group itself would probably decide how to go on. In workshops of one or two weeks, the 'symbolic group' may remain on the walls and be available for further projection, changing aspects of each person and so on.

With patients who are not very articulate, this project can provide an exciting channel for expression and communication through the paintings. The outline body shape gives safety for those who require it; whereas the more adventurous can take liberties with the boundaries. (See Figure 9 for an example of the variety of images resulting from this project.)

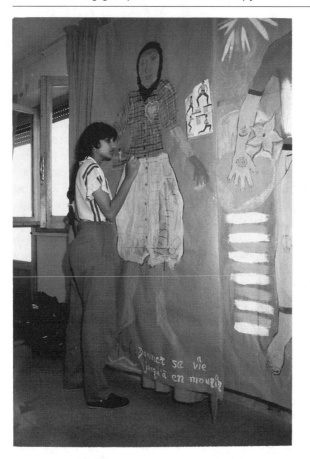

Figure 9 Body image

Small group themes

This is a very flexible project and often follows on well from 'body image' in a short-term group. According to the number of people in the group, they divide into small groups. There would usually be around four to five in each. The project is simply to decide on what to do in that group. I might introduce a few limitations such as, use the clay, discuss what you are going to do with the group beforehand, but otherwise it is entirely up to each group. Some groups have lengthy and profound discussions and decide to make a group project, others speak briefly then go straight into making, others decide to work on their own image, etc. Sometimes the groups are competitive with the other groups, and sometimes the members of each small group admit to feeling competitive within their group.

Depending on what has been going on before in the group, it might happen that small groups are formed by people choosing each other – which can produce fears about being left out (someone said, like being chosen last for team sports at school), or sometimes names are drawn out of a hat. Whichever way it happens, there is useful material to work on (see Case Example No. 7). In one workshop, the groups chose each other on the basis of knowing each other previously; then later they decided to move around and work with people they hadn't met. So the small group projects can continue for as long as the group decides. If names come out of a hat, it can feel like being in your family: you didn't have a choice. If you choose people, you are then responsible for getting on with them, or not.

These small, sub-groups contain important elements for the group as a whole and it is useful to have periods when the whole group is together to reflect on the process.

Group painting

I have never actually suggested that a group make a painting together but this has often been suggested by a member. If it happens right at the beginning, I would simply query why the suggestion has emerged then. Perhaps it is an attempt to make the group cohere very quickly? If, after thinking about it, the group decides to make a painting together in the first session, the results are often a bit stilted and 'polite', and each person keeps to their own area of the paper. Sometimes a group painting will happen when members have been working on their own or in pairs and is a way of bringing the whole group back together. It can also be suggested when the group is in conflict, as a way of trying to resolve the conflict by working together. A group might decide to work on a painting for several days, or weeks, and the painting will become a visual history of its life and process (see Case Example No. 3).

Group sculptures

There are times when a group might be reflecting on itself, and the individuals on their role in the group. It may be helpful at these times to make models of the group as the individuals see it. Working spontaneously with, say, clay, can produce some very powerful representations and lead on to discussion about the family. The group may then decide to sculpt their family. One example of this happened during a weekend interactive art therapy training group in Bulgaria.

There had been much discussion about families, which was somewhat intellectualised. At my suggestion this time, the members made sculptures of their family out of clay. They were completely engrossed in this process.

When everyone had finished, they sat back and started to talk about their own (verbal) patient groups, in which people were very reluctant to talk

Figure 10 Clay model of family group with a stork and mask

about their families. They found this irritating and could not understand why this was so. The discussion continued for some time, very intellectually, with much reference to family therapy literature, etc. I noted that they had not talked at all about their own sculpted families. After the break, we reassembled and I made this observation. Someone said, 'Let's start talking about our families!' This was an attempt to 'do what the conductor said' but when it came to the point of starting, nobody wanted to speak. We sat in awkward silence, a rather gloomy atmosphere in the room. Then someone pointed out a feature of someone else's family and how they felt about it. I said it seemed easier to project one's own feelings onto another's family sculpture and perhaps they would find it easier to do this. The person whose family was being discussed was at liberty to correct, add something or be silent. The group came to life at this point and moved around the room, sitting in front of another member's family, projecting freely and receiving plenty of feedback from the rest of the group. After some time, we reflected on what had been happening and some important insights emerged.

In Bulgaria, family networks are essential to survival. They are extensive and many generations are included; third and fourth cousins are known and valued. For example, if you want to visit another part of the country, you check to see if a relative lives there. If so, you will stay with that relative and not in a hotel. The family exists to help and support each other and forms a layer underneath 'the State'. It is where real interaction takes place. Therefore, it is inadvisable to speak critically of any member of one's family,

Figure 11 Clay model of family in a ring

as you do not know if they might at some time have a connection with a member of the group. To acknowledge a problem in the family to strangers would be to lose face. These strong interactions served a vital purpose during the five hundred years of Ottoman rule in Bulgaria. Non-relatives may be adopted as family and are then subject to the same protections. In the Caucasian republics, where there are similar cultural features, a host is obliged to protect his guest while that person is in his home, so strong are the laws of hospitality. These are very deeply ingrained responses and although things are changing now – families are split up, urban living has taken over from country life – the group members felt the force of them during the workshop. They were not sure, for instance, of my role. Was I actually a member of the (equivalent to) KGB and would spy on the group and report on their families? Were there members of the group who would do this? That issue was never resolved – but the members realised very clearly why their own patients had problems in discussing their families and were much more in sympathy with why.

See Figures 10 and 11 for examples of work produced: in Figure 10, the family is shown on the left, with mother the large figure in the middle around whom the rest of the family revolve. She has somewhat octopus-like arms. The family is frequented by a stork (which traditionally brings babies and good luck) and a mask has been included to show how the family hide themselves behind an inscrutable mask. In Figure 11, the family is shown together in a ring, but outside is a dead sibling. A spoon has been included as a symbol of food and hospitality, and a hat which could act as protection if necessary.

I have described this particular incident to show how powerful such a theme can be and how it can develop in unexpected ways. The same can be said of most projects and themes: they can provoke much powerful emotion. The fact that there are objects to contain these is an important element in art therapy, but the objects can take on a life of their own and be invested with enormous ritual significance.

I conclude this brief exploration of themes and projects by mentioning that I have found the study of anthropology and particularly of cultural artefacts and their ritual significance has been valuable to me as an art therapist. The importance of ritual in our lives is often lost or played down. In art therapy we may find it again.

Chapter 7

Short-term interactive art therapy groups

Art therapists have traditionally been employed in large psychiatric hospitals where they have often worked with groups of in-patients on acute admissions as well as long-stay wards. They have tended to run so-called 'open groups', which consist of a studio-type room into which patients may wander at various times of day, sometimes painting, sometimes not. Alternatively, 'projective art groups' may be held, where one-off themes are set by whoever happens to be running the group. Often this is not a qualified art or group therapist. In either case, little attention is paid to the dynamics of the group.

Conducting groups in acute admissions wards has been seen by most workers as difficult, given that the patient population changes frequently and patients are very disturbed and often heavily medicated. Yalom, in *Inpatient Group Psychotherapy* (1983) points out that workers are generally only familiar with the long-term model of groups (based on groups in private practice or out-patient groups consisting of well-functioning individuals). Currently, there is no coherent, commonly accepted method for running in-patient groups so there is often confusion and ineffective conducting, whereas it would be possible, by adapting the model, to run short-term interactive groups.

Such groups as there are in acute wards are often run by non-trained personnel. There is competition for time and the groups are not taken very seriously. Sometimes they are set up without full knowledge and permission from the ward administration and this can lead to tension and even sabotage. In my experience, art therapy groups are no exception and art therapists have reported being frustrated by the ever-changing population in the 'open' groups which they have felt obliged to run.

Yalom's research on the effects of groups run on three different wards in different institutions revealed, not surprisingly, that the more highly the group is valued by all the staff, the more effective it is for the patients. If a group is run by non-trained staff and seen to be less important than other activities on the ward, patients will feel it is not worth making a commitment. What usually happens in such groups is that they are held irregularly, there are many interruptions and cancellations, the task of the group is not clear, doctors, nurses and other staff may 'call out' their patients from the group. In those wards where the group is valued, patients sense this and gain greatly from the experience. To achieve this much attention must be paid to timetabling (which needs to be agreed by all staff) explanations to colleagues and firmness in establishing the boundaries and the task of the group.

In psychiatric units catering mainly for the acutely ill, the trust and cohesion that are important elements in long-term groups are impossible to attain in the short term, due to the instability of the patient population and greater disturbance and poorer functioning of most participants. Yalom (1983: 32) drew the conclusion from his research that group therapy is an effective treatment on in-patient units. It demonstrably improves outcome, and patients treated in hospital are likely to go on to out-patient groups. Major modifications of the 'long-term' technique are essential, and the technique must be fitted to the type of patient population.

Yalom firmly believes that it is worth the difficulties involved in establishing an interactive small group. The great majority of patients have come into hospital bedevilled by chronic interpersonal problems – e.g. isolation, loneliness, poor social skills, sexual concerns, authority problems and so on. The therapy group gives an ideal opportunity to explore and correct patterns of behaviour which had led to misery and hospitalisation. Patients can be helped to understand how their behaviour prevents them from developing their desired interpersonal relationships (Yalom, 1983: 33). Art therapists, with their long experience of working in acute wards, are well suited to take on the challenge of running groups. As we have seen from Chapter 4, there are particular responsibilities involved in this task. The physical arrangements of the room and the kind of art materials used are an important influence. Whereas it is possible to be flexible about individual sessions, a group must be carefully timetabled. In a hospital unit there is the question of escorting a group of disturbed patients from one part of the hospital to another, requiring active co-operation from other staff, particularly nurses. However carefully the art therapist informs other staff of the time and place of the group, it is seldom possible to adhere to the given times.

Despite the problems likely to be encountered, some art therapists have tried to run 'closed' groups for a limited time. For example, in 'Art therapy in practice' (1990) Drucker describes her work with psychogeriatric patients in a setting where neither art therapy nor group work (other than social skills) was a usual form of treatment. She mentions that in working with the elderly:

There seems to be an emphasis on doing things to and with older people – rather than just letting them be and do for themselves, and allowing them to set their own pace and explore from within, even if it doesn't reach staff expectations.

(1990: 94–5)

She felt that both individual and group art therapy could provide a space for such exploration.

As far as the structure of the groups was concerned, she generally ran 'open groups', but there was one group which was an exception to this:

the same eight people (two men and six women) remained in the group for a period of six months consecutively. I shall not describe each individual within the group but instead how they changed within the group dynamics.

(1990: 99)

Drucker points out that because of the high anxiety level, she 'needed to be directive for the first couple of sessions so that anxiety would not get the better of them' (1990: 99). By the middle period the group had become cohesive and noticed if someone was missing: 'There was a feeling of belonging and caring.' At the end, some of the patients were discharged to a variety of out-patient social groups. Drucker concludes that the elderly people were able to use the structured art therapy sessions to express their feelings, explore their difficulties about 'being old', and share together or confide in her.

Getting through their resistances and insecurities about not being able to draw or paint resulted in opening up expressions of negative and positive feelings. It also gave these people an opportunity to have a sense of belonging, and I felt privileged to belong with them.

(1990: 102)

Art therapists seem to have an additional difficulty in setting up 'closed' groups in that the profession is still relatively new and many staff have little idea of the nature of the process. Art therapy groups can suffer from a mistaken notion that they are 'recreational' despite much groundwork by art therapists in explaining about the groups to the staff. Molloy (1984: 7) makes this point in relation to an individual session in a rehabilitation ward, although it could equally well apply to a group in an acute admissions ward:

I remember conducting an individual art therapy session with a patient in the side-room of a rehabilitation ward. The patient was engrossed in his painting when two men from the hospital works department walked in saying 'Excuse us'. They then made a brief inspection of the plumbing and went out again. As they left one of them, who recognised the patient, came across and said, 'Hello Bill – doing some sketching. That's nice.' The whole incident was over in less than a minute, leaving me angry, distracted and wondering if I would ever be able to get reasonable boundaries established, as this sort of casual interruption had happened many times before.

Molloy goes on to say that he was able to explore this with the patient usefully afterwards but nevertheless, persistent interruptions were very destructive. When he reflected on the incident, he found it difficult to direct his anger appropriately as staff were following a system that had always prevailed. He concludes:

> That is why it is so important to get psychodynamic work and thinking into rehabilitation departments. Until staff have experienced the power and depth of such work, they will simply not believe in the effects that seemingly casual actions can have upon it. Art therapy is particularly effective for demonstrating this . . . If they [staff] can follow a series of paintings and see how a patient's internal world is deeply affected by the intrusion of seemingly trivial events, then they may begin to become more sensitive in their interactions.
>
> (1984: 7)

Rapid turnover is inevitable in an acute admissions ward where by the nature of the ward, patients stay only a short time. The patient may only attend for one or two meetings, there is no time to work on termination in such a short space of time, and there is usually great disturbance in the patient group – for example, psychosis, substance abuse, acute alcoholic crisis, anorexia, severe depression, suicidal tendencies. Patients are, as the name suggests, acutely uncomfortable and in despair. They are generally not seeking personal growth or self-understanding but looking for ways to alleviate their distress. Often they receive medication and are discharged when the crisis has passed. Many of the patients in the group may be unmotivated, ambivalent about attending, having come because they were 'sent' by their doctor. The therapist has little time to prepare or screen patients so has minimal control over group composition. The group is unlikely to become cohesive (an important curative factor); there is no time for a gradual recognition of subtle interactions among members or for working through these, and no chance to focus on transfer of learning in the group to situations outside.

The primary goal of the therapist then, must be to engage the patient in therapy. The group aims must be realistic and relate to the patient's current state. All, or most of, their problems cannot be solved during a stay in acute admissions.

Anxiety is one of the most over-riding emotions for the majority of patients. Going into hospital is itself traumatic and the patient probably feels ashamed and 'weak' and even 'crazy'. He or she sees people who are looking strange and acting in a bizarre manner and is frightened by this.

Anxiety, depression or another acute state may have the result of rendering someone incoherent. They might well be confused in speech and manner. They are certainly not in a frame of mind to contemplate long-term personal growth!

An art therapy group can offer an alternative to verbal groups or to endless sitting, smoking, watching television, heavy medication. The art therapist has to be persistent in acquiring time for a group as it may be seen, as in the example given by Molloy, as a way of passing the time and not very significant. Yet art therapy can provide a valuable means of communicating for patients who are deeply distressed, whose grasp of reality is somewhat tenuous, and for whom coherent verbal interactions in a group would be difficult or impossible.

Molloy says (again of rehabilitation) that the art therapist will need to make constant efforts to show how art therapy can be valuable to staff, too, in providing insights into individual and social pathology which would not otherwise be available (1984: 7).

There are, according to Yalom (1983: 14–19), complex issues around who leads an in-patient group and a wide range of professional disciplines are represented by in-patient group leaders. The debate about group leadership is often a debate about power, prestige and professional territory rather than leader competence. However, most disciplines receive no training in groups in their professional lives. Art therapists can at least claim that they have been regular participants in training groups throughout their Diploma studies and in Goldsmiths' at least, there is much emphasis on the ability to conduct a group effectively and in an interactive or group analytic style.

So how does the conductor cope with a group in which the membership may change from day to day? The focus must be on the 'here-and-now' for that is all the group may have, and on how members relate to each other in the group. Focussing on the there-and-then – for instance, why a patient came into hospital, his or her life problems or complaints for which he seeks solutions from the group – is not useful. Such problems cannot be solved by the group which leads to demoralisation of the group and thence to loss of faith in the group process. It is not helpful for a therapist to try to establish a common theme as this often results in a very 'intellectualised' discussion which may or may not relate to most group members.

The group leader must, then, turn the attention of the group onto its own process and encourage interactions. In other words, he or she must be more 'active' as there is no guaranteed 'life' for the group outside that session.

Yalom feels that many therapists fail to focus on interaction because of their lack of training in traditional group methods. The ability to facilitate member-to-member interaction and to help members learn from observing their own process is an acquired therapeutic skill that requires group training and supervision rarely available in most professional educational curricula (1983: 23). He also suggests that many therapists are frightened by an interactional approach, and this would appear to be borne out by the literature on art therapy groups where there is an emphasis on individual art productions and discussion through the medium of the painting rather than using the paintings in a more direct, interactional manner. There also seems to be an assumption that because people are homeless, drug addicted, have had psychotic episodes, are mentally handicapped, they are incapable of sustaining this approach.

On discussing patients who are having psychotic experiences, Yalom suggests that psychotic patients may be made worse by non-directive leaders who focus on insight rather than interaction. On the other hand, a carefully thought out small group can provide such patients with the only possible place where efforts may be made to ameliorate their disruptive behaviour. In the therapy group the ward members can offer the patient constructive feedback in carefully modulated doses about the effects of his behaviour on them. It is the task of the therapist, Yalom says, to create an atmosphere in which feedback can be perceived as supporting and educative rather than attacking and punishing (1983: 64).

Sometimes even the most acutely psychotic patients are able to offer accurate and important observations about other members of the group – they can do this much more easily than they can receive feedback. Patients in a psychotic state have ready access to primary processes which can be expressed spontaneously through art materials. They can express feelings, thoughts and fantasies in a way that other, more defended patients, may find reassuring or liberating. All patients have frightening, incoherent feelings or fantasies and the ability of the psychotic patient to identify and express these may actually be more reassuring than frightening (1983: 65).

Nevertheless these groups are often characterised by considerable disruption, interruptions from within and without. Psychotic patients are often restless and not able to stand the whole session. Patients who suffer from a lack of inner structure are often highly threatened by being thrust into a situation that seems to be out of control. It becomes difficult for the therapist to impose a tight structure on the group and, at the same time, provide a level of work that is meaningful for all patients, whatever their level of functioning.

The aim of a group for patients who are confused, anxious and have short attention spans might be to provide support and facilitate communication. This would have a different structure from a group which aims to explore and analyse feelings. It would not threaten fragile defences and is less challenging.

CASE EXAMPLE

An in-patient, interactive art therapy group, held twice weekly, on an acute admissions ward, was attended by twelve patients. There was a core of eight who had been together during the past two groups, one in the previous week, and one early in the week, and four new members. The group was held in a disused side ward and had plenty of art materials and space available. The conductor saw her role as trying to encourage the group members to find a way to communicate through the materials, paying attention to how they felt in the here-and-now. Several of the patients were receiving medication. One of the new members, R., wanted to talk about his problem with his wife, whom he blamed for all his life problems, including his admission and recent suicide attempt. He spoke in a loud, whining manner and tried to engage the conductor in a one-to-one relationship, ignoring the other members, including the three new people who had come in with him that day. One of the older members asked him 'What does she look like, your wife?' and he started to describe her, whereupon the member said: 'I'd rather see a picture of her', in an attempt to bring him into the group 'culture'. Reluctantly R. picked up some felt-tipped pens and began to draw, half-heartedly. One or two members made straight for the art materials and got on with something of their own or sat watching. R. got stuck and looked around the group for inspiration. He started to draw J., a young woman who was passively sitting, staring into space. She said 'Stop staring at me, I don't want to be your wife.' Then she covered up her face and started to cry, sobbing 'No I didn't mean it . . .' L., an older woman who had joined the group with R., got angry with him, saying she didn't want to be in the same room with him. The conductor suggested she might try to draw herself in relation to him, in an attempt to keep her in the group. L. cursed a bit under her breath but went on to draw him as a fat worm and herself as a blackbird. He was shocked and said that was how he felt about himself in relation to his wife – that she was always about to peck him and eat him and he was powerless to do anything about it. He really did seem to take on the characteristics of the worm. Other members were intrigued by this sense of powerlessness in relation to women and some had actually produced images of being helpless. One woman had drawn a huge white-coated figure towering over a tiny female figure. She said, 'That's how I see doctors and all doctors here are men. Men are the problem, not women. Women have no power.' (That morning she had learned that a doctor she had grown attached to, a Registrar, was about to leave and she was very upset and angry.) I. produced her painting which was covered in red blotches: she said, 'That's what my husband gave me, he beats me up.' R. thought she was insinuating that he beat his wife and said that he had never thought of such a thing. In the meantime he had doodled a large block of wood which covered the faint drawing of a woman he had started earlier on. The conductor mentioned that he had drawn the idea of 'beating up' i.e. with a large block of wood, or alternatively, crushing. Did he want to crush I. at that point? Referring the issue back to the group, the conductor wondered if the alternative to being helpless was seen as crushing or other violent behaviour. She was aware that some of the in-patients had histories of giving out or receiving violence, for which two had been in prison before. She also wondered if, as female conductor, there was a sense of her being 'all-powerful'. P. intervened quickly and felt that she could not tolerate R.'s picture and wanted him to change it so that the female figure was sitting on top of the block and not being crushed by it. He said: 'Do it yourself' offering his painting to her. She held back, there being a 'taboo' on interfering with others' work which the core group members had been operating. He said: 'Go on, I dare you.' She snatched the picture and painted a large, strong-looking woman sitting on the block. She said: 'There, she's sitting on you!' He said: 'You are just like my wife, always sitting on me, always using me like a *** prop. I can't do anything. She's a dead weight but I can't get rid of her.' She said, 'Well, you told me to do it for you! You're the dead weight if you ask me . . .!'

The interactions among members continued throughout the group with the conductor drawing attention to overall themes. By the end of the session, male–female power relationships had been explored even by some of the most incoherent members as a result of their paintings. Despite the angry exchanges among people who hardly knew each other, there was also plenty of humour and some group members had obviously gained useful (if painful) feedback.

Clearly, conducting interactive art therapy groups with patients whose grasp of reality is, at least at times, very tenuous, requires much skill and confidence and support from other staff in the institution – not least for the conductor, who is likely to be extremely stirred up by the material of these intensive groups. It goes without saying that training and regular super-vision is essential.

Chapter 8

Group interactive art therapy with children and adolescents

In many centres responsible for the care and treatment of disturbed children and adolescents, the aim is to get the children back into school and to their homes, if at all possible, so that the worst effects of being in an institution are avoided. There are therapeutic communities where group work is the norm, but in child and family centres and schools, it can be difficult to establish a group for various reasons: timetable, group work not being part of the 'culture' whereas individual work is, the children not being in the centre for more than a few months. Sometimes it happens that there is nobody on the psychotherapy staff with group work expertise. So the only groups that the children participate in are in the classroom, where the task is to improve their school work. In the majority of placement centres where our postgraduate art therapy trainees do their art therapy practice with children, it has been up to the trainee to introduce group work. This has often been difficult to set up and has ceased once the trainee finishes. The reasons for having a group with children and adolescents are much the same as for adults. It is a very different experience from being in the classroom.

Foulkes and Anthony, in their chapter 'Psychotherapy with children and adults' (Foulkes and Anthony, 1965) make the point that age and natural group formation to some extent dictate the therapeutic techniques used with children and it is essential that therapists familiarise themselves with the developmental phases of childhood and the sequential changes that occur in the child's intellectual, emotional, social, moral and linguistic spheres. This presupposes, they suggest, a good understanding of child psychology and development as a background to group therapy with children (1965: 190).

There are many similarities with play therapy, especially when working with very young children, and it is obvious that the therapist needs to adapt his or her technique and language when working with different age groups. Foulkes and Anthony recommend about 30 to 40 minutes per group, twice a week. Art therapy would seem to offer an excellent opportunity for interaction as children readily use materials, and do so spontaneously, except in rare cases where they are very withdrawn and inhibited and need special encouragement.

Interestingly, the most recent book about art therapy and children in Britain: *Working with Children in Art Therapy* (Case and Dalley, 1990) focusses almost entirely on individual art therapy sessions. In *Art Therapy in Practice* (Liebmann, 1990), one group with children is described by Trish Fielden, a psychotherapist and art therapist, who gives an account of an art group with dyslexic children in a school for children with learning difficulties.

This group was set up for the given reason that the 'resource of individual therapy was both relatively expensive and scarce', rather than because of any obvious acknowledgement of the value of groups in themselves (1990: 104). Fielden's hope was that the group would establish its own identity and that its members would encourage their peers to join in. There was a problem in getting the children to join the group, in that art was associated with formal art lessons and therapy was an unfamiliar or threatening term to most pupils. It might also have been that the group was seen by staff as a 'poor relation' to individual therapy and not highly rated.

The group was entitled: Self Expression through Art'. It appeared to be 'informal' and emphasis was on the individual child's experience rather than on interaction or group dynamics. Fielden says:

> At first I spent my time working with individuals, engaging with the process as it emerged from sharing their pictures, clay models, scribbles or forlorn and angry attempts at self-expression. As the group gelled, more of this sharing happened in the group.
>
> (1990: 106)

Despite the initial justification for running a group (that it was 'cheaper' and more children could be accommodated than in individual therapy) the group proved an important place for shared communication. The 'curative' factors of the group went into operation. Fielden reports:

> Some individuals may need encouragement to stay with their discoveries, and support to integrate these into their lives. In the group the kind of 'games' we all play in defence of our feelings can be captured, shared, examined and maybe discarded. Group interaction is an important part of this learning, which for the group described, then needs to be transmitted into the everyday life of the school.
>
> (1990: 110)

Linesch (1988: 133) an American art therapist writes more positively about group work:

> It has been suggested by some that group therapy is the modality of choice with the emotionally disturbed adolescent . . . Group therapy, as one component of a multimodality approach, does have an important role to play in the treatment of troubled youngsters. However the

selection of group therapy, either alone or in combination with other treatment approaches must be responsive to the needs and conflicts of the particular adolescents involved.

She goes on to say that group therapy with adolescents is often difficult and draining for therapists and can even become countertherapeutic and destructive. Harnessing the adolescents' creativity and expressive potential, as in art therapy, can, however, direct and sustain positive interaction.

Linesch quotes Blos (1962: 210) who considers that group therapy is important for adolescents because it helps the adolescent to separate out projective components of their behaviour from objective facts. This happens within the contained environment of the group, in which the adolescent can safely wage his or her battle with authority figures.

Linesch concludes that since the struggles of adolescence revolve around self-expression and peer interaction, it seems obvious that a combination of art and group therapy techniques will be particularly effective with this population:

> The group modality touches the needs of the adolescent and the art modality facilitates the group process. It is a complementarity that is both curative and exciting and underlies the effectivness of the group described in the remainder of this chapter.
>
> (Linesch, 1988: 135)

She then goes on to describe her group of four adolescent girls who had difficulty with self-expression and peer interaction. All had experienced abuse and neglect and their behaviour was aggressive and hostile. They met once a week for eighteen months, as a closed group. Linesch used an interactive approach to the group, drawing on Yalom for her theoretical structure. She began by asking each girl to introduce herself by making a collage. She structured the first four sessions to introduce the girls to the art materials and help them understand how the materials could be used expressively. She points out that, although the four girls all knew each other from living together in their centre, the group gave them an important new interactive arena and the fresh introductions emphasised the sense of beginnings (1988: 136).

Linesch found that the art process allowed discussion of the here-and-now of the group process: diagrams, symbols and metaphors allowed the adolescents to distance themselves from the potential anxiety in this task (1988: 142). Transference issues were also able to be explored through the art materials. A central feature of the adolescent state is the struggle with his or her own separation and individuation, so the transference interactions with the group leader may be particularly powerful. Often the adolescent is resistant and hostile towards the therapist and there is a tendency for 'gangs' to form to defeat the therapist. The art materials give the members an opportunity to express these feelings indirectly and safely. The art objects themselves give the group a focus for exploring and reality testing their relationships with the therapist.

Of course, peer relations are of central importance to adolescents and the interactive art therapy group gives ample opportunity for these to be explored.

The following case example, with young adolescents, shows how, even in a very short-term group (four sessions) much useful work was done.

WORKING WITH A GROUP OF YOUNG TEENAGERS

The following case work was carried out by an art therapy trainee, now a fully qualified art therapist. She did her art therapy placement in a school for children with communicational and emotional difficulties. Group work was not normally used, timetabling problems and lack of enthusiasm among staff being reasons given, but T. felt that the children would benefit from an art therapy group and decided to try to set one up.

She found many difficulties for reasons already stated: timetable complications, staff ambivalence, lack of understanding on the part of the children of the benefits they might gain. The only period of time available for the group was 45 minutes, once a week, for four weeks. After hesitating about starting with such unpromising conditions, she decided to go ahead and five children, aged between 11 and 14, committed themselves. In discussion, we felt that a focussed, theme-centred interactive model would be most useful, given the limitations surrounding the group. T. reported as follows.

Week 1

The theme for this session was to make portraits of each other, using objects, shapes or colour. The group were quick to start, Ann, John and Lyn waiting to see what Sue and Fred[1] would do, as if taking the lead from them.

I experienced the group interacting very soon into the session and was rather surprised at the free rein of emotions which were expressed. They did not seem to hold back on their feelings. Laughter was used to cover up any embarrassment which they felt concerning the fantasies that were being portrayed in their portraits. A feeling of competitiveness to see who could make the funniest picture became evident in the session.

Fred portrayed the group most honestly and fully, giving the group plenty to laugh at, but also showing them how much thought and sensitivity could be given to such a theme. An example of his observation on Lyn was to cause the most poignant and demonstrable feelings in her and cause the group to reflect and feel his honesty and her reaction.

He had used her name to pun with his picture, drawing a house which smoked through the chimney. He had given her many rooms, one of which he had left empty, as he explained that it represented the part of her brain which she did not use. Lyn became adamant in telling the group that she did not smoke but was so angry to be seen as an empty room that she stood up, faced the wall with her back to the group and gave a monologue as to how she did not like her name being taken in vain. There was complete silence, as if the group were frightened to see what would happen next. I voiced this fear and Fred continued with real sensitivity, explaining that Lyn's house was made of strong red brick. That it needed to be strong to contain her strong feelings. This comment seemed to explain a lot about how he found Lyn. The group were now in fits of laughter.

It was now John who decided to talk about his pictures. He was laughing so much that he could not begin. I asked him whether he was too scared to start because of the strong reaction in the group to Fred's descriptions. This seemed to acknowledge what was being felt in the group.

The theme had allowed for all sorts of fantasies to be explored. They had been quite volatile: Sue and Lyn responding directly to their feelings. Laughter had persisted throughout the session. I felt exhausted after the group, as the level at which they operated amongst themselves had been confrontative, and much energy had been exerted in dealing with these feelings through their laughter.

Week 2

They were asked to choose partners and then make an object in clay together. These would be kept secret until the end of the session, at which point they could then guess what each team had made.

The feeling in the room was quick to change to one of competition, as the girls went into one group and the boys in another.

The two teams decided on making an object each. Each team knew what was being made by the other member of the team. As the session progressed, the teams tried to guess what each were making. There was a feeling of great excitement in the air as the objects were being made.

Lyn had instigated the idea that they each make their own object and that they should be related to containers. Sue had tried to get the team to make something together, but Lyn would not agree. Ann made a vase, Sue a casserole dish and Lyn a basket. Lyn's was the largest of the objects and she had made sure she would use up all the clay, hence a new bag of clay which usually takes a year to be used up in the art therapy department took three-quarters of an hour to be used. I felt that this seemed to express symbolically Lyn's neediness to the group, and her need to be in control.

Fred and John had agreed to make monsters from the film *Ghostbusters*. John had twice tried to instigate them both making something together, but Fred would not agree.

I drew their attention to the fact that they had not directly stuck to the brief and asked them why. Lyn quickly replied that she felt that there would have been arguments if they had made something together. So the element of competition had not only existed between the two teams but also against each other. I felt that the issue of hierarchy was very much being battled out between themselves. Lyn was the most forceful, but the boys tenaciously tried to keep themselves separate from her.

The objects appeared to be stereotyped. The boys made monsters and the girls containers. The objects suggested that the boys were more into overt fantasy than the girls. They managed to guess what the girls had made. The monsters, on the other hand, were more difficult to guess as they wanted the girls to guess which film they came from. The elements of hierarchy and competition were much enjoyed and this was acknowledged by both teams.

As time was short I explained that we would start the next session by talking about them. They expressed their enjoyment at having made the objects and said they would like me to bring them in for the fourth week so they could paint them and take them home.

Week 3

I began by asking them to choose another person's object and say what they would add to it.

Lyn chose Sue's casserole dish which she said she would add some food to. This became the container for the group to deal with the issue of hierarchy. She said that she would then cut me up into small pieces, add me to the dish with some poison, which she would then feed to Sue. Fred instantly replied that if she was to do that then they would have to kill her as they could not have her (Lyn) leading the group. The casserole dish was the vehicle for their fantasies of hierarchy to be symbolically dealt with in a direct way which seemed very primitive and overtly cannibalistic.

John had been left with Lyn's basket. He did not want to choose it, so he chose Ann's vase instead. As Lyn's basket had not been chosen, I asked the group if anyone would like to choose it. Lyn quickly opted to choose her own, but Sue responded saying that it could be used as a shopping basket. John very quickly replied that of course it could not, as it was far too heavy already.

The group did not hold back on their feelings and, in being so direct and honest, they seemed to be able to break down barriers that could stop a group from moving on.

The theme of the session was then given, which was: to choose a name out of a hat, thereby choosing a partner at random. Once chosen, the theme was to draw around your partner, and think about how they would like to be

Figure 12 Two figures from a young people's group

seen, so that you then fill in the shape with this in mind (see Plate 3a and Figures 12 and 13).

Sue and Ann were chosen as one group, John, Fred and Lyn in the next group. Lyn did not seem to be wanted by Fred and John. They took a long time deciding who should draw around who. The whole process of drawing around each other was very embarrassing. Whether it was the issue of Lyn being the only female and having to draw and be drawn by one of the boys and vice versa seemed all too difficult for them. Their physical boundaries were being tested and therefore the theme of the session seemed to be lost. What remained was their difficulty and having to come to compromises which were difficult. The actual process seemed to be what was crucial here in this session.

The session was to go on into the fourth week. I was asked again to bring in their clay objects so they could paint them and take them home.

Figure 13 Two figures from a young people's group

Week 4

The group were to finish the portraits. They could then choose what they would like to do.

The portraits were very soon finished and then talked about. There was some avoidance in this, descriptions were kept on a very safe footing and spoken about in terms of colour and what they wore. Maybe the leap to visualisation had been too difficult. I certainly felt that they had not really used their imagination. The session felt very rushed. Maybe because there had been so much to fit in, in such a short space of time. They all chose to paint their clay objects as soon as they could. I said that we would keep five minutes at the end to discuss their feelings around the sessions and how they felt about the ending.

Lyn, who had involved herself emotionally, seemed to express her difficulties. She had twice outside the group tried to tell me that she had

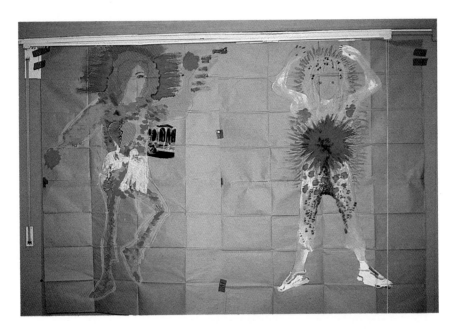

Plate 1a Different body images

Plate 1b Body image

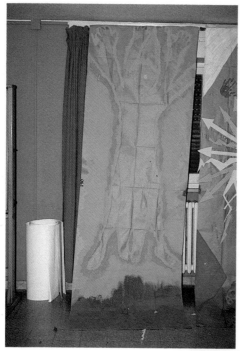

Plate 2a Body image

Plate 2b Body image

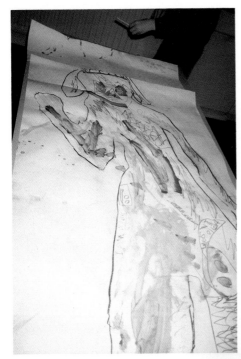

Plate 3a Body image from a young people's group

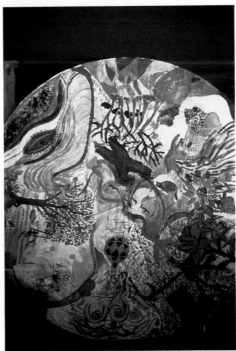

Plate 3b Group image, including dolphin and vulture

Plate 4a Making an environment for self-boxes

Plate 4b Making an environment for self-boxes

Plate 5a An example of an environment: 'childhood'

Plate 5b An example of an environment: 'secret room'

Plate 6a The power of the State

Plate 6c The eye of the therapist

Plate 6b The psychiatric hospital

Plate 6d Group as a train

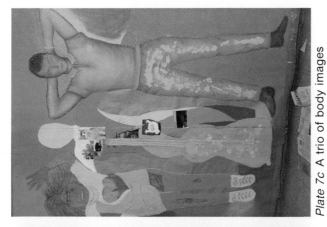

Plate 7c A trio of body images

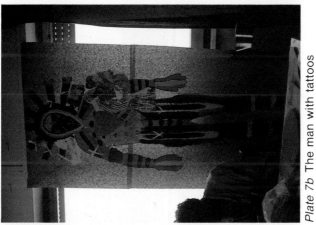

Plate 7b The man with tattoos

Plate 7a Devil mask

Plate 8a Henrietta

Plate 8b Environment with plants

missed swimming, and again in this last group, expressed the same thing. I acknowledged this, saying that I realised that she had felt that it had been very brave of her to last the four weeks. John said that he had valued the group immensely, had found it fun and wished that it would continue. Fred had commented on punctuality, stating that he too valued the group. (It had been Comic Relief day at the school and John had arrived five minutes late but had apologised, saying he really had not wanted to miss the beginning.) Sue and Ann also voiced the wish that they would have liked the group to continue.

Summing up

Over the four weeks the group dealt with many issues concerning hierarchy and competitiveness, the testing of boundaries, and the process of interaction through their fantasies and difficulties with one another. They were able to contain their strong feelings through the art and also to express themselves directly in the contained space of the sessions. I feel the process of art therapy with an adolescent group manages to deal with many issues which in normal circumstances might be difficult to confront. They managed to do so symbolically through the art, which was by no means easy, as was shown by the interaction with Lyn and Fred. The artwork in the adolescent group seemed to provide a safe container for many feelings. There had not been many silences, and each group member seemed to play a very particular role in the group. This had been challenged: for example, in week three when partners were chosen at random to work on life-sized portraits. Emotions ran high yet they managed to survive their difficulties.

I would have liked a longer time for the sessions – maybe one and a half hours. There did seem to be a rush to fit in as much as we could into the sessions. However, due to the school's timetable this had not been possible. I also feel that the theme-centred approach had worked well, giving the group a safety. Had there been more sessions, it would also have been interesting for the group to have experienced a more 'non-directive' approach. It was the consensus of the group that they would have liked it to continue.

This case study shows how much is possible even in a few short sessions. The children were able to benefit from the intense interaction which the group stimulated and it positively influenced the way they later behaved in the classroom.

It is a pity that there does not seem to be more appreciation of the value of interactive art therapy groups for children and adolescents, at least if we go by the literature and experiences of trainees on placement. Children who are very shy and withdrawn and attract bullying could benefit from being in a safely contained interactive group, as could children who are aggressive and badly behaved in class (to give two extremes). A knowledge of group dynamics would seem to be invaluable for all teachers, yet surprisingly little time, if any, is spent on this during teacher training. Art therapists trained in groupwork could give much support to teaching staff, as well as to children, in schools and centres for care and treatment of children and adolescents and this is an area of work which needs to be further researched and developed.

NOTE

1 These are not the real names of the children.

Section II

The model in practice
Case examples

Introduction

When preparing this book, I spent a lot of time trying to decide how to incorporate the case examples. Should I intersperse them among the theoretical sections of the book or put them all or most of them in one section. I decided to put the majority into this section, but have cross-referenced so that theoretical points made earlier on can be illustrated by easy reference to a case example.

Included in this section are case examples from training groups which constituted elements in introductory or ongoing art therapy programmes, from mixed staff–resident workshops in a therapeutic community, and from patient groups in different settings. My role as conductor obviously changes according to the function of the group, although there are many features in common between training groups and patient groups.

When preparing introductory courses which contain experiential art therapy groups, I am careful to structure the programme so that these groups are firmly contained: that is, participants have plenty of theoretical and small group discussion periods to process the material. As will be clear from the examples, the dynamics of interactive groups are powerful. Herein lies their effectiveness in teaching trainees about the process of group art therapy: either for groups or for individuals.

The same precautions apply to patient groups: as others have confirmed, much care needs to be taken in ascertaining that the patients themselves and other colleagues are clear about the nature of the group; that they don't think it is 'recreational'; that they are aware that patients will be stirred up by the process and that this can be positive, requiring support and understanding from other staff and not increased doses of medication.

One aspect of working abroad which I have had to get used to is having an interpreter present throughout the training groups. This was a strange experience at first, not being able to communicate directly with participants. I did not want to specify that people should speak English as not only might this requirement exclude people in their own country, but it is difficult to express oneself at a deep level, unless one is more or less fluent in a foreign language. It is better to have an interpreter, and then we are all 'in the same boat'.

As my knowledge of some languages increased, and as a result of having everything repeated from one language to another, my 'passive' understanding improved and I was at least able to understand some of the verbal interactions during the art-making process as well as in the discussion periods. But in some cases (e.g. Greece) I understand nothing of the language and find this extremely difficult and frustrating. It has made me realise how devastating it must be to be deaf and/or dumb. I gradually got used to making spontaneous remarks in the feedback sessions (and hearing these interpreted!) and indeed we have been very fortunate in having interpreters who are interested in and sensitive to the art therapy process. The interpreter becomes a member of the group with an essential function: if she or he isn't there, it is as if the group is 'stuck' until we begin to make the best of our lack of communal language. The interpreter is rather like a co-conductor!

Art therapy is not a 'non-verbal' process – or at least, only in the image-making part. This does not mean that images have to be transcribed into words. On the contrary they have their own life and direct emotional response. But there is an interaction between the visual and the verbal, and this is what I miss when I don't understand the language. I would not have been without this experience, though, as despite the frustrations, it has taught me much about the complexities of communication, as well as improving my knowledge of the languages in at least some of the countries I've worked in.

I want to stress that these examples are not presented as: 'the best way to run an interactive art therapy group'. Rather, they are examples of the way in which the process of the group has developed and the way that I, as conductor, and the group experienced them. My own theoretical background and personal perspective obviously influences my selection of issues to focus on. But the material of each group is so rich and there are so many levels of verbal and visual interaction going on, that the ways of interpreting what is happening are endless. I still find, several years later in some cases, that I discover something new when looking at the photographs and thinking about the processes. This is exciting and I hope that this element in group interactive art therapy communicates itself to the reader.

Case example 1

Rooms and materials

ROOM AND MATERIALS: I

I was asked by the director of a therapeutic community treating drug and alcohol abuse to run an introductory art therapy course for his staff, which included many people from other countries training in methods of treating substance abuse. I gave an outline for a week-long programme which included several experiential (practical) workshops. I described the method I would use and the materials needed; the maximum number of participants to be twelve.

I met the director. He explained it was the first time that art therapy would be introduced and everyone was excited. He asked me to take thirty trainees, as had been the case with previous courses (e.g. psychodrama). I explained that my approach, which was experiential and required working with art materials (something the participants had never done), was not suitable for such a large group. I could present a seminar or lecture to a larger group but the course participants would be limited to twelve. We compromised on fourteen.

I said we should need a large room as people would move about. Also that it should not be carpeted as it could get messy. Water should be easily available. I gave a list of materials required for the practical workshops.

On arrival at the centre two days before the course, I found I had been allocated sixteen participants and an interpreter. The room was the main seminar room for the centre, complete with carpet, chairs with folding writing block and one or two small tables. The nearest water was in the kitchen, a few minutes walk away. It was exactly the kind of room which should be kept clean and tidy and which was totally inhibiting for our purpose!

I checked with the staff at the centre how far I could go in reorganising the room, beginning with removing the carpet. That was agreed. I asked for several old tables, newspapers and plastic sheeting for the floor, plastic buckets, a mop and a large amount of rag. There was very little wall space uncluttered but I checked the possibility of blue-tacking and pinning paintings to walls and curtains. I set up two tables in an accessible part of the room and began to lay out the materials. Unfortunately, even though the person who had acquired them had been identified as an 'artist', the materials were far from appropriate. There was a large roll of graphic design tracing paper, children's watercolour sets and tiny brushes, some oil paints and pastels, small packets of instant-dry clay. There were also scissors, kitchen knives and spoons and plastic water pots as requested.

I thought: I have two days to get materials for sixteen people together in a small town in the mountains or possibly with a quick trip into the city. I was annoyed with myself for not having been absolutely specific as to my needs. It was clear that the 'artist' had his own ideas as to what the materials should consist of. It was my own fault for not being absolutely specific.

First, I raided the kitchen and stores at the centre for paper plates, kitchen towels, cardboard boxes, packaging, string. I found cling-film, wrapping paper, plastic cutlery in the stores along with discarded polystyrene chippings and packing. I asked staff to bring in old magazines for collage. A visit to the town revealed a well-stocked stationers with plenty of coloured tissue paper, ordinary white cartridge, parcel paper, sellotape, charcoal, coloured pencils and felt-tipped pens. There remained the problem of the paints, so a visit to the city and to a decorators shop was necessary to buy a huge can of white emulsion, powder colours, house-painting brushes and wallpaper paste. White parcel-wrapping paper was obtained by the office – enough for all sixteen participants to make life-sized paintings. The one problem remaining was the clay but this had been promised for the first workshop.

By this time the staff and residents at the centre had the feeling of something distinctly strange about to happen.

ROOM AND MATERIALS: II

I was asked to run a series of art therapy workshops over five days for psychiatric staff of a large hospital in Bulgaria. I limited the group to eight but on the day fourteen turned up, including one visitor from a hospital over 200 miles away! The room, an office in the department of psychiatry, was big enough for six people to work in comfort so we had to extend the boundaries by going out into the corridor and on one occasion into the garden (through the window). The weather was extremely hot. There was a small washbasin in the corner (it was a consulting room). The room had the advantage of no carpet and nothing on the walls so that they could be covered in paper and used to paint on. It was also ours for the week, so work could be left undisturbed. The room reflected the crowded conditions in which Bulgarians in the city are obliged to live and work and this issue emerged many times in the group.

As for art materials, I suggested we take a look at what was readily available in the town and especially in the area around the Medical Academy. We have to bear in mind that packaging is not a feature of this economy and that things we take for granted in Britain (plastic bags, foil, cling film, string, lavishly illustrated magazines) are hard to come by. There is a chronic shortage of building materials. It is not a 'throw away' society, at the moment, anyway.

We discovered the following without going into the 'artists' shop'.

2-Dimensional

mark making materials such as pencils of varying thickness, soft, hard, black or coloured
felt-tipped pens and ticket markers of varying thickness
biros
crayons
pens and ink
charcoal from the traditional charcoal burners
conte crayon
lipstick ends
decorators' brushes
paint rollers
printing ink

Paint

(essentially a pigment containing glue)
tempera – egg white as the glue
children's paint boxes
acrylic wall paint
decorators' colours in tins or packets of raw pigment
glue to mix with this
emulsion or oil-based gloss (latter not recommended because of drying problems)

Surfaces

(any flat surface not too absorbent)
cardboard from boxes
fibre board
old packing paper
newspaper and newsprint (ends of rolls available from Print Union)
wallpaper
backs of posters
'sugar' paper from toy shop

coloured wrapping paper from florists
brown paper from post office

Ready-mades

magazines for a store of images
old posters
newspapers
unwanted photos

3-D

boxes of various sorts from hospital store and supermarket
newspapers for papier mâché
toilet roll centres or cardboard tubes
remains of exhibition displays (friendly museums and trade centres)
plaster of paris (from hospital store)
bandages (these may not be easily available as medical supplies are precious)

Clay

No problem in Sofia or anywhere there is a ceramics factory or local potters
working; or brick works; may be dug up and prepared; impossible to obtain
in certain areas – e.g. coast.

Junk

A large box of odds and ends; included packaging material, leftover bits of
fabric and leather, pine cones, beads, bits of wood, toys, remains of broken
transistor radio, old car parts, old clothes, polystyrene blocks, broken
necklaces, sequins, dried-up fruit (especially prunes) and other objects
which appealed to people's imagination.

wallpaper paste
scissors
old knives
spoons
plates
plastic cups
yoghurt jars for water

Fabric

remnants obtainable from dressmaker, factory
bits of leather from shoe factory

Figure 14 Conference room, Medical Academy, Sofia (used as art therapy room)

old clothes wool (expensive but can also use nylon or acrylic fibre); visit
   farms for fur and wool
cotton wool (not always obtainable)
string
shoe laces (cheap)
feathers from local market
straw from farmyard

Very difficult to come by was scotch tape (sellotape) but heavy brown parcel
tape could substitute.

Figure 15 Studio at Netherne Hospital in the 1950s

It was more difficult to find materials when we worked on the coast, but there were: sand; stones; driftwood; irreparably torn fishing net; and a more plentiful supply of old posters could be found in addition to many of the items above. Hotels had a good supply of cardboard boxes.

Part of the value of an art therapy group is in the collection of and experimentation with materials. The enhancement of creativity is an important aspect of art therapy and the interaction between members around the art materials and their subsequent mastery of image-making in different dimensions was an important learning experience for them.

Figure 16 Attic and greenhouse, Torvaianica Therapeutic Community

Figure 17 Hut used for art therapy workshops, Art Psychotherapy Unit, Goldsmiths' College

ROOM AND MATERIALS: III

This was the first of a series of week-long training programmes in art therapy in Bulgaria. Participants were mainly psychiatric personnel, over half of the fourteen being doctors.

The room assigned was in the Institute of Hygiene, which as its name suggests, was not accustomed to having art activities on its premises. We had been given the Conference Room as a base because it was the biggest room in the building. So the issue of size had been acknowledged. The room was thickly carpeted with a long table in the middle covered with a green baize cloth. There were armchairs along the length of the table (about twelve on each side). At one end was a space for hanging coats and behind this a washbasin and cupboards. At the other end was a clear space with a blank wall behind it. There were several advantages: the size, the washbasin, the blank wall space. The problems were: the huge table and its green baize cover, the armchairs filling the room, the thick (obviously new and precious) carpet.

The first task with the group was to reorganise the room and make it habitable for our purposes. We removed the green cloth and discovered several smaller tables making up the large table (see Figure 14). We moved these around the room, immediately creating more space. We determined a sitting area and moved the armchairs there and piled the rest up in a corner. We designated the area round the washbasin the materials and cleaning up corner. We obtained several large sheets of plastic and covered the carpet and remaining floor space completely. We put newsprint on the tables (which had metal tops and thus were washable).

The space was thus transformed from a very formal conference room to one where many different kinds of interactions were possible.

Figures 14, 15, 16 and 17 give examples of the kinds of rooms art therapists might use. Figure 14 shows the main conference room in the Institute of Hygiene, Sofia, subsequently converted into a group interactive art therapy studio for one week. The studio at Netherne Hospital, one of the first hospitals to employ an artist (1946), is shown in the 1950s in Figure 15. (Grateful thanks to the hospital management of Netherne Hospital for permission to print this photograph.) Figure 16 shows the attic, Torvaia-nica, near Rome, and Figure 17 shows one of the huts used by the Art Psychotherapy Unit, Goldsmiths' College.

The unwilling participant(s)

Transference, countertransference, projective identification and all . . .

I am often asked to deliver intensive introductory programmes in countries where art therapy is not established but where there is willingness and intention to do so. For practical reasons, the programmes usually last for a week. Mostly the participants are professional workers and can be given 'time out' for this period. I emphasise that I believe that a combination of theory and experiential work is the most effective method of learning about the art therapy process and that I use a group interactive approach to teaching and conducting experiential groups. I also emphasise that the introductory programme is not designed to enable them to practise art therapy afterwards but to enable them to understand its potential as a treatment modality. Some may wish to go on to further training of course.

This way of working is unfamiliar in many countries, as I have come to realise. Terminology familiar in one place is not in others. I quickly realised that, in one centre I was working in, 'workshop' meant 'seminar' – that is, a verbal description and demonstration of the fundamentals of art therapy, whereas I meant an involvement of the participants in the actual process of working with materials in a group. This was naive on my part, but fortunately could be sorted out before the course started and people were eager to become involved in a 'hands on' experience. I am now very careful to point out that active participation in the process is part of the course and that the experience is almost certain to stir participants up emotionally. Therefore, as participants are usually selected by directors of training, heads of department or hospital chiefs, it is essential that, in so far as they are able to predict, these selectors do not expose people who are likely to be damaged by the course.

Unfortunately, it still happens that people join the course who are seeking a lecture format and to be told 'how to do' art therapy on patients. Others are coming for personal therapy. I have found it important to spend some time in individual discussion with each participant prior to the course to establish their aims and expectations. It is worrying that some people do not read or understand the course description beforehand, such is their enthusiasm to attend. Appreciating that it is possible to want to know 'how to do it' and acquire some personal insight at the same time, it still concerns me lest the purpose of the course has not been understood. The case study which follows is based on an early experience I had of presenting an introductory short course in art therapy to a conference of art teachers over a weekend. It took place in the UK. I have included it because I think it is one of the worst fears beginning (and perhaps even experienced!) therapists have, that is, of people walking out of the group or ganging up on the conductor.

A group of art teachers at a conference were offered a short course in art therapy as part of the conference programme. There were other workshops available, such as 3-D design, curriculum development, photography. The short course consisted of a lecture and discussion on the general principles of art therapy and two practical, experiential workshops. The nature of both inputs was clearly described. The lecture was to the whole conference but the workshops had to be selected. Two groups of eight persons had opted to do the short course workshops (2 hours each). One of the groups consisted of eight people, six women and two men, plus myself. I decided to present an 'open-ended theme' and, having pointed out the materials available, invited the group members to make a visual introduction of themselves – putting in those aspects which they felt fairly represented them and using colour, shape, collage, etc. to do it.

One man, P., who had previously let us know he was in an advisory position in the art education world, objected immediately and vociferously to the surprise of other group members. He declared that he had thought the workshop was going to be a continuation of the lecture and he had several questions to ask me. I was very new to running workshops and my heart sank at his extremely aggressive stance. I pointed out that this was a chance to experience the process, albeit for a very short time and in highly structured conditions and I hoped it would illuminate some of the points raised in the lecture. It was up to each participant how they presented themselves. There was much unease in the group and whereas previously people had seemed eager to try the task, now they sat glumly, staring at me and waiting for me to do something (or so it seemed). I remained quiet, hoping very much that he would relax. He said 'This is a waste of time. I propose that we continue the discussion from this morning.' He was joined by a woman who felt my suggestion of making a visual representation of herself was 'stupid and childish'. She delivered an angry lecture about the perils of the advertising world and was surprised that I had given a theme which seemed to be asking people to advertise themselves. At this point I wanted to escape very much. I was tempted to say 'OK, let's have a discussion!' I felt the kind of rumblings familiar from adolescent groups, when a gang is about to form and try to demolish the conductor! Looking back on this situation, I wish I had had the experience of Yvonne Agazarian who might have said something like: 'Anyone else here want to join this sub-group?' As it was, I was desperate for someone to start working with the art materials, fearing a mass walk-out, and indeed it was the man's wife (I found out later in the group) who reached for paper and felt-tips and said she wanted to try the task. He was by now furious and demanded she stop. She looked from him to me and put down her paper. Some other people picked up paper and crayons and began to draw.

I reminded him, and at the same time, other group members, that they did not have to remain in the group if it really was not what they wanted. He could choose to leave. Or he could choose to do nothing. He said it was now too late to go to another group and that in any case he had wanted to continue the discussion about art therapy. It was clearly obvious that nobody wanted to do this stupid task, so why did I not get on with the discussion? He felt he wanted his 'money's worth'. I was in danger of getting drawn into a fight for by now I was getting angry and, being inexperienced, felt responsible for the 'mess' the group was in. I could have taken up his 'ambivalence' as representing the group's but I did not dare. In fact, I didn't even think of it, as I was so overcome with anxiety.

I sensed though that other group members were getting a bit tired of this aggression and were feeling left out. They all looked fed up and disconsolate. I could not have cared less whether they did the task or not at that point and just sat without saying anything further. He then revealed his considerable authority in the art world and declared that he was disappointed in art therapy if this was what it was about. I began to understand that a big power struggle was going on. I remembered that the group were all art teachers (I hadn't actually forgotten but in being taken so by surprise by the hostility I experienced I had temporarily put this information aside) and that they were probably experiencing divided loyalty. He was determined to hold onto his power in the group even if it meant rubbishing me.

I was feeling much panic and was not sure if it was mine or the group's (probably both). I swallowed hard and said that it might be difficult to be in such a group where you knew people outside and did not know what might come up in the group (I had said in the lecture that people were often surprised by images they made and how they were affected by them). I supposed that as teachers they were expected to know what was going on and it must be strange to be in this situation where they were not at all sure what was expected. I didn't add that they might feel like children at school but in fact one woman burst into tears and said she had experienced me like her head teacher who always made her sit on a low chair when she went into her study, while the head sat on a high chair. When I'd mentioned visually introducing herself, she couldn't think of anything; her mind went blank and she literally 'wiped herself out'. Other people joined her, saying they were undervalued by society, being teachers. Some said they thought they should be artists and not art teachers and that they had 'failed' by going into teaching. Someone said that being an art therapist *must* be more interesting than teaching.

P. sat in stony silence, with his arms folded, representing a stern authority figure, apparently scornful of the self-revelations. I realised that he could see himself as losing face if he joined in. He was, apparently, powerless to leave. The male–female power clash was centred on ourselves and right up till the end of the group, he sat like that. The tension emanating from him was almost unbearable and not even his wife could reach him.

I repeated a comment about the unfamiliar process of art therapy, despite image-making being familiar to the group members, and drew attention to the way that members had felt themselves like children. One woman commented 'I feel trapped in teaching but I can't do anything else now. It's too late.' Someone else said 'I thought art therapy was supposed to make you feel relaxed!' (I had certainly not given that impression in the morning's lecture . . .) I suspected that P. was feeling both these feelings but he was not about to admit it and I was certainly not going to suggest it. He, through being stuck in a role (lecturing) wanted me to remain in that familiar role and when I did not, became angry and, moreover, scared. He then tried to lead the group into demanding I take that role and when the attempt failed, withdrew into silence.

The group came to an end with some people having doodled with crayon and felt-tips. It had been a most uncomfortable and painful experience and afterwards I felt exhausted and somewhat deskilled. It was only in reflecting some time after that I realised how much this reflected how the art teachers felt most of the time, but asking for support seemed to them 'weakness'. It was acceptable to 'learn about' art therapy, but being in the group had offered a chance for lowering defences, desirable but terrifying at the same time.

The next day (it was a residential conference) I learned from one of the organisers that the group had gathered together in the bar that evening and talked animatedly about their art therapy experience, P. included! We had not talked about the images at all. A group of art teachers had avoided the image-making process ('wiping out' their art) but the presence of the images 'in abstract' had seemed to lead to some insight about their personal situations outside the group and how these had been reflected in the group. They had also engaged in some 'conductor battering' which might have relieved angry feelings about authority.

Case example 3

Developmental processes in a group painting

I conducted a group interactive art therapy training workshop over a period of one week during a residential conference open to health care workers, including practising art therapists.

As the conductor of an ongoing group, in which firm boundaries, interpersonal relationships and group dynamics are central features, I found it important to clarify my own personal boundaries during the week. It is clearly impossible that members do not meet each other outside the group, and obviously I shall encounter them at breakfast, lectures and at social events where I will have a different role from that in the group. I feel, however, that within this model of training it is necessary to remain in a fairly 'formal' relationship with group members – exactly as I would if working in a therapeutic community where I would see patients outside small groups and would even, perhaps, be preparing a meal with them. I feel it is important that the group can use the conductor for transference purposes, and even though in an interactive group the role of the conductor is less opaque than in an analytic group, the conductor is still available for projection, transference, etc. It can be confusing if the conductor is intimate with one or two group members (e.g. drinking with them in the pub) during the life of the group.

I shall describe a situation where maintaining my 'role' was important, where both the group and myself had to negotiate some tricky boundary questions, and where the group clearly demonstrated a developmental pattern of birth, latency, adolescence, adulthood and death.

On the third day of the group, which consisted of eight members, four men and four women, several members wanted to make a group painting following the suggestion of one member. I drew attention to the eagerness with which the group followed this suggestion, made by one of the men in a very positive and enthusiastic manner. They did pause to reflect for a short time but were determined to work together on a painting. They took some time discussing how to make the painting and what shape the paper should be. They decided to make a very large circular shape and about half an hour was spent in preparation of the paper, cutting, sellotaping, deciding who would work where, etc. There seemed to be some verbal discussion but much non-verbal signing about who was to be next to whom. I felt like a teacher or a parent watching the children at play. They worked freely and energetically, splashing paint but staying in their own territory. Eventually a dolphin emerged in the centre of the painting. There were flowers, trees, fruit, birds and sunshine – altogether a joyous, happy atmosphere prevailed. There was much giggling and chattering. I was more or less ignored, but felt I had become the dolphin in the centre. The group continued to paint almost to the end of the session. There was a sense of innocence, rather like the Garden of Eden.

On the next day, the group assembled in a sullen mood. Some members looked angry and there was a sexual charge. They decided to return to the painting and some dissatisfaction was expressed with it. The dolphin stayed but two members began to paint what looked like a vulture intertwined with it. There were attempts to cross over boundaries and invade territory. Adam and Eve appeared and snakes coiled round the trees. It began to look menacing. The group were totally absorbed in the painting, walking on it, moving across it, changing images and arguing with each other.

From time to time, members would glance across at me angrily. I felt very uncomfortable, hot and in the way. I wanted to shift my position and walk round the room, but felt rooted to my stool. The imagery filled the room, sexual, aggressive, yet contained on the large circle. There were still remnants of the previous day's work, notably the dolphin which now appeared to be wrestling with the vulture. I wondered if I was the dolphin 'rescuer' and the vulture 'devourer', rather like Kali in Hindu mythology, and representing the division in the group between male and female power, positive and negative forces and other dualities which may have been present. I did not put this to the group at the time lest I interrupt the intensity of the painting.

Several minutes before the end, I drew attention to the approaching time boundary and asked group members if there was any reaction they wished to share before we finished for the day. Most expressed being totally absorbed in the painting and feeling a bit stunned at what had come out. They went away quietly.

That evening there was a social event involving much drinking of alcohol and discharge of much emotion through disco dancing and possibly some sexual activity. I stayed on the edge of the event, feeling slightly ill at ease about the effects of the event on the group members. I knew that powerful feelings to do with adolescence and sexual awareness had come up in the group that day. It felt like a teenage party, such was the intensity of the drinking and rather manic activity. I wondered about the wisdom of having such an 'officially organised' event during a conference containing much psychodynamically-oriented experiential study. As far as my group were concerned, I felt a bit like a parent being excluded from the teenagers' party.

I felt a spoilsport but nevertheless avoided attempts by the group to pull me in. The process of the group was very strong and we had much to work through in the remaining days of the course.

Most people arrived on time next morning, tired but willing to work. The sullen mood of the previous day had lifted and people expressed dissatisfaction with some of the things done the day before. They negotiated how to improve the situation and worked again on the picture. It was as if some of the adolescent feelings of the previous day had been discharged – partially in the painting but also, I suspect, acted out in the social event.

I wondered if anyone would discuss the party. They did not. Much seductive interplay had gone on the day before and also at the party. They discussed feeling tired. They did not talk much but set to work on the painting together, making some quiet comments and suggestions to each other. I felt they might be a bit embarrassed at the rather violent imagery of the previous day and were attempting to smooth it over. It certainly felt quiet in the room as the painting entered its third day of being. I said very little and the workshop ended. I noticed that the vulture and the dolphin had hardly been touched yet they were intertwined as opposed to wrestling.

On the final day, the group assembled and sat for several minutes in silence. They discussed the possibility of continuing with the group painting but decided against it. One person said he wanted to do a painting on his own and others agreed. They did not move, however. Then a discussion began about the painting and about the week in general. I was asked to comment and give my impressions about the workshop. They wondered about my role and how it felt not joining in the painting (perhaps a reference to my not joining in the party, or at least not wholeheartedly!) Without my giving comments, members started to discuss my role and how they felt about the approach. I was perceived as 'laid back' but necessary to the group's functioning. I made a comment about the dolphin and the vulture and wondered if my perception about them representing two aspects of the conductor/mother – rescuer and devourer – was shared. Members spent some time contemplating this, and the likeness to the Garden of Eden of the picture. One member asked what would happen to the picture and the rest of the workshop was devoted to discussing each person's contribution and how it had formed 'the group'. A suggestion came that the painting should be photographed with us all holding it and there was unanimous agreement that this should happen after the end of the workshop when a camera could be found.

The person with the camera who offered to take the photo then said she would send copies to all participants. I commented that this was one way in which the group could be prolonged – that we were not actually facing the ending which was rapidly approaching. This seemed to give permission for members to feedback to each other and myself and the group ended with a rather sad silence.

Afterwards, we did take photos of the painting. The organisation of addresses and contributions to costs was done by two members and in due course, the photos arrived.

I have often wondered how the group process would have developed had the social event not taken place. Given that the participants were not patients, and the advice not to meet outside the group could not apply, it is possible that the group boundary was maintained. I think though that important learning for the participants may have been lost by their 'acting out' features of that day's group, rather than coming back to experience and exploring them through the painting and in the contained space of the group. I have offered some suggestions here about the painting (see Plate 3b) in the context of the group's development. It is a piece of work which contains numerous layers of meaning and which could have been worked on by the group for many weeks, if not months. Note the dolphin and the vulture in the centre of the painting.

Case example 4

Life processes in small group environments

I had the idea during a three-day training workshop in Greece, to ask the participants to continue working with their 'self-boxes' by dividing into three small groups of four and making an environment for their boxes. They selected who they wanted to work with and went to different parts of the room. One small group then decided to go into the ante-room where all the materials were kept. They announced this to the rest of the group, saying that people should get materials out straight away (which they did without much protest!) Then they shut the door, thus effectively cutting themselves off from the rest and from myself, unless we chose to open the door and enter. Nobody did.

Group 1 decided to suspend their boxes from the ceiling. D. had the idea of making a mobile so they fixed some string across the room to hold the boxes. First they suspended A.'s box, which was full of cotton wool, then took a pole and fixed F.'s and N.'s at either end. D. (the only man in the group) put his box in the middle 'for balance'. He called out 'This is the balance of power' (see Plates 4a and 4b).

Group 2 created a 'play room'. They fixed large sheets of paper on the wall and painted a nursery. They made a shelf and put toys and the TV set in. They cut out paper dolls and filled the space with scenes of childhood (see Plate 5a).

Group 3 remained a mystery. There were many comings and goings and laughter. At one point, they went out of the building (breaking the boundaries), it transpired to buy a tape of music. It was interesting that Group 3 had blocked the materials off (the 'goodies' provided by the parents) as well. With the whispering and laughter coming from behind the closed door, there was a strong feeling of sexuality – taking over the parents' bedroom, perhaps.

At the agreed time to finish the art-making process, the groups visited each other's environments. The main focus was Group 3. They had created a sensual environment, complete with candles, dishes of burning incense, a tape of sultry music was playing (Arabic music). An incredibly dark, secret and seductive space. A skirt was draped on a chair together with a mask and crash helmet! Other members felt the sexuality of this space and someone described it as 'forbidden pleasure'. It had a hypnotic, Eastern feeling to it and another comment made was that it was like a very early Greek or Byzantine setting (see Plate 5b, but this is taken in daylight and does not reflect the sultry quality of the environment).

In the discussion which ensued, T. pointed out three stages of man: childhood, adolescence and adulthood. D. said it was 'play' and 'play' in Greek also means 'toy' and 'game'.

I wondered how it had happened that the three groups had decided what to do when it seemed the grouping was fairly random. Sharing the men was an issue because Group 3 had two men and two women behind the doors, contributing more to the notion of secret sex. Members said that in Greek society, it was difficult to have relations with the opposite sex if they were not intended to lead to marriage. It is still a society in which women find it difficult to feel equal to men. The issue of 'secret sex' was therefore very pertinent to the group.

It was stunning, though, how different phases of development had been represented unconsciously by the groups as there was no prior discussion between them and they were not aware of what each was doing until the end.

Of course there were many other issues to be discussed from these small groups, such as the decision-making process in each group, working together, the presence of the conductor and so on, let alone the rich metaphoric and symbolic content of the imagery and its meaning for each member.

The following day the group worked together to de-construct the environments and this in itself was an important process. The small room, in the daylight, had lost its seductive power and became once more an ante-room for materials. The group had taken in and used its symbolic meaning on the previous day: the objects had been internalised during the highly emotional discussion about sex and its particular meaning to the participants, so what remained could easily be de-constructed.

Images of the group

Spontaneous images of the group often arise during art therapy workshops. They are often linked to preoccupations of the group at that time – with the conductor, with their lives outside, with their interpersonal relationships elsewhere on the course.

CASE A: 'THE STATE'

During the final stages of a block training programme for medical personnel in Bulgaria, one member produced Plate 6a, which he described as a symbol of 'the State'. It is a huge bulldozer which is about to crush two small people. They are standing rather precariously on top of two spheres which are themselves perched on somewhat fragile bases. The image is complex because the two people could be the intended future co-ordinators of the art therapy project or the two conductors or symbolic of male and female about to be overcome by the power of the group or the larger society outside.

The group were preoccupied at this time with the first phase of the training coming to an end. It was a very new venture for Bulgaria at a time when people felt themselves at the mercy of bureaucracy and 'the State'. The group discussed the image and they were concerned that their new-found insight and enthusiasms (represented by the male and female conductors as they saw the two figures) would be crushed once the training had finished. They did not know if they had sufficient skills or ability to make the necessary changes in their situation to practise art therapy. The bulldozer was built to be heavy and difficult to move but it only has to move a short distance to crush the figures. The figures are holding out their arms – as if they could be offering a welcome to the heavy machine or on the other hand, asking for help. Someone said that perhaps the machine would stop there and leave the figures safely 'on top of the world'.

CASE B: THE PSYCHIATRIC HOSPITAL

This image (Plate 6b) was made by four doctors, preoccupied with their role

Figure 18 Group as a fountain and bullring

in society. They were not sure if they were the rescuers or wanted to be rescued. They have made a personification of the hospital, which they said was more like a prison. They did not know if their role was custodial or therapeutic. The 'head' of the hospital has a red cross hat on (symbol of rescuer) and a large ear, which could either be used for listening sympathetically or listening in order to punish. They wanted their role to be therapeutic but felt constricted by what they experienced as that particular society's expectations of psychiatrists.

It also felt as if the walls of the hospital were a safe container and perhaps it was easier for everyone to stay in that situation rather than risk 'breaking out'. There were further discussions about the role of 'the State' and its protective as well as restrictive aspects.

The group discussed their perceptions of psychiatry in their own country and in 'the West'. They saw more scope for using therapeutic skills in the West, but they were also very keen to change things in their country. There are similar elements in both A and B, in that 'the hospital' is both imprisoning and containing, and the 'bulldozer' is threatening but potentially merciful (i.e. it hasn't squashed the figures, yet). There was transference to the conductors in both structures: they were both powerful yet vulnerable. The group were unsure whether the conductors were going to 'listen sympathetically' or imprison them through divulging information to 'the wrong people'.

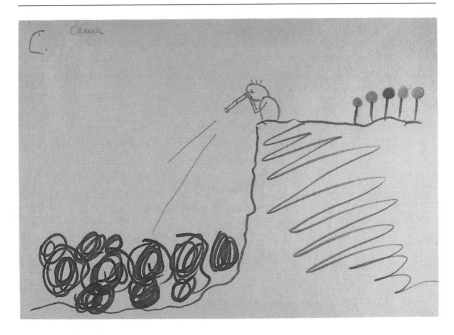

Figure 19 Conductor spying on the group

CASE C

The group in Plate 6c has been portrayed as a life belt. Art therapy is symbolised by the brush (which someone said was like a penis). The group is also on top of the life belt which is actually 'the eye of the therapist'. So the group is in the eye of the conductor where it will be kept safely. There is food on the life belt and the group can survive until it is eventually rescued.

There was a powerful pull on the conductor to 'rescue' the group and strong feelings about the 'freedom' of the West as opposed to the 'imprisonment' of the East.

These images from the examples A, B and C illustrate how individuals' personal experience links into the group's experience of each other and the conductor and their experience of the society 'outside'.

Plate 6d and Figures 18 and 19 show images of the group, made in small groups using clay. Plate 6d shows the group as a train, and the participants going on a journey. The model tells a story of the group; it symbolises coming out of the tunnel (unconscious) and into the light. The members of the small group told the rest of the group what the passengers had seen on their journey.

Figure 18 shows the group as the fountain of life and a bullring. It can be a place of peace and tranquillity and nourishment, or a place where violent scenes take place. There were many other symbols meaningful to the makers of this model, to do with their life in Spain and South America.

Figure 19 shows the conductor standing on a cliff, looking down at the group through her binoculars. The member who made this picture had a feeling that the conductor could 'see everything'.

Case example 6

Catharsis

This example is taken from a short-term training group aimed at introducing art therapy to people working with substance abuse. The group, which consisted of twenty people, some staff and some residents of therapeutic communities in Italy and South America, had been working in pairs on life-sized portraits of each other (see description of body images, pp. 63–8). In the interaction I shall discuss, one of the men was a priest and the other a worker in a closed community. Both came from South America and were training in Italy.

One of the men, S., had been very nervous from the beginning of the week and was always anxious to 'do everything right'. He felt himself to be very clumsy and indeed his whole bearing was unconfident and hesitant. This applied to his painting of C. which he worked on carefully and with much checking out with C. to see if it met with his approval. C. also put a lot of care and thought into S.'s painting. He was having a lot of difficulty with the feet and asked S. to stand close to the painting so he could make the feet right. By this time the feet had gone decidedly wrong and were out of proportion to the body. They were also two left feet. This would not have been important in itself except that it was obviously causing distress to both men. At this stage in the group, all the pairs were intensely involved in the process with their partner but the tension between S. and C. was communicating and some people went over to offer advice. Eventually C. drew a pair of feet which although looking awkward, satisfied him for that moment. Several minutes later I observed S. moving to get some paint. He passed by C.'s water pot and somehow the dirty water got knocked over and spilt all over C.'s careful rendering of the feet. There were gasps of horror all over the room. C. looked distraught and S. sat down, put his head in his hands and cried. I felt an intervention was important and between the three of us we concluded that it would be possible to place a clean piece of paper over the lower part of the legs and re-do the feet. In fact, C. decided to paint the feet and stick them on and they certainly looked more sturdy and in better proportion. (This is an example of how reparation can take place symbolically through reworking a painting when it has 'gone wrong' in the eyes of the painter.)

When the group as a whole paused to reflect on the process so far about an hour later, S. said he had something very important to tell the group. He was flushed and excited. He said he had suddenly remembered an incident from his childhood. One day his mother asked him to go down to the village to fetch the day's milk in a large pitcher. He was thrilled at being entrusted with this task. On the way back, however, he tripped, fell and broke the pitcher. He lost a whole day's milk which was very precious and expensive. His mother was furious and beat him, calling him a clumsy fool. He was so ashamed and humiliated at failing his mother in this way and it seemed had spent much of his life atoning for this accident. When he spilled the water over C.'s picture of him, he felt overwhelmed with shame. He felt he had destroyed something precious which C. had given him. It was a very moving moment in the group. It was true that S. had been experienced by several members as irritating because of his somewhat obsessional manner. He was also inclined to want to control the group. It was quite incredible that the accident with the water had brought back an incident which he had repressed most of his life. From that moment of catharsis he was able to relax much more, joining in the 'play' of the group instead of being on the outside.

The symbolic re-enactment of a deeply repressed trauma through the process of image-making and interaction with another is not entirely unusual in such a group.

Another example happened in an introductory art therapy workshop I was conducting for a group of medical personnel. All the group spoke good English so I was able to interact freely with them. Several members in the group of twelve were ambivalent about being in a practical workshop and would have preferred more lectures. They were also ambivalent about art therapy as a treatment process. It was not a profession in that country and some of the participants still believed it was a form of 'arts and crafts' which kept patients happily occupied, despite having had a lecture and seminar on theory and practice.

I had stressed that people should wear old clothing, or overalls for the workshop, as the art therapy process can be messy. However, some turned up in their white doctor's coats and others in smart clothing! They were engaged in a similar task to the one described above, although I had modified it slightly because the group was a 'one-off'.

Two men worked together but I noticed that one of them, J., although starting off his painting by discussing and observing his partner, had become engrossed in painting a very careful portrait of someone looking completely unlike either his partner or himself (sometimes – indeed often – people make the portraits as they see themselves). He had withdrawn into the painting and worked fast, as if he had a vision of the person in his head. At a point when everyone had finished the paintings, I asked them to fix them on the walls and invited them to say how they had experienced the task. I did not invite them to speak about the paintings themselves, although that was quite possible if people wished.

J. immediately said he was shaken by what had happened to him. He said he had not wanted to come to the group as he thought art therapy was 'not serious' and he had no talent in art at all. He also felt that, as a psychiatrist, it was strange to be in a group where he had to paint. However, he was a little intrigued as he had heard a lot of people talk about art therapy so that was why he had come. When he started to make the life-sized portrait, he found himself painting someone who used to be his best friend, but with whom he had quarrelled over a girl when they were first in college. The quarrel was very serious and was never resolved. Shortly after, the friend was killed in a car crash. He had blotted out the pain of all this but it came flooding back while he was painting. Although his partner in the group was not much like the friend, there were some similarities and he thought it was for this reason he had created a true likeness of his friend. He cried in the group and said he would never have believed the power of art therapy. The group were very moved by this and he felt supported and liberated by the cathartic experience. He said he felt he could now mourn the loss of his friend.

It was important during the discussion stage of the workshop for me to refer to this incident which clearly illustrated the power of the art therapy process and the necessity for clear boundaries and adequate time and space for processing the material which often arose. The participants, who were mainly psychiatrists and psychologists, were no longer under the illusion that art therapy was to be taken lightly, or that they could offer it to patients without having proper training themselves.

Power and domination
Clay workshops and sub-group themes

The group divided into four small groups, people choosing who they wanted to work with. The experience of the life-sized portraits was still active and the 'symbolic group' now occupied the walls of the studio. The task was to use the clay in any way the small groups wished.

In Group 1, five members from the closed community had chosen to work together. They had a brief discussion and I noticed that B. had made a suggestion which appeared to be accepted. The clay was pounded with much enthusiasm and loud banging. A structure was created with a wall around it. There was much arguing followed by scooping up of the clay and pounding it back into a large block. Then the group sat contemplating the ball of clay and each other. B. again seemed to take the lead and was offering a suggestion which was accepted. Everyone took a piece of clay and started working individually. Then they joined B. who had flattened out a large piece and was shaping it. I saw they were making a mask, using elements of the painting which A. had done of B. earlier on.

When they were satisfied with the structure, they began to paint it. Normally, clay needs to dry, be biscuit fired and painted with special underglazes, fired again and glazed. There was no possibility of carrying out this procedure here so it was 'good enough' to use the acrylic paints for the purpose. The group were preoccupied with the painting, especially B. who was clearly enjoying himself.

In Group 3, it seemed that individuals had chosen to work on their own pieces without much discussion or interaction (see Figure 20).

In Group 4, people also worked individually, although they had spent a lot of time talking before using the clay (see Figure 21).

When the making process was complete, groups visited each other and a discussion began. Group 1 explained that they had started by making a prison but they themselves felt trapped by it and wondered why they had chosen the topic. They thought it was because their community was 'closed' and they had chosen each other and chosen the topic for this reason. They felt resentful of the other group members who were not in this position. They'd decided – or rather B. had suggested – making a 'devil mask'. They

Figure 20 Small group themes: making individual objects

Figure 21 Group talking and making

Figure 22 Group making a 'welcome house'

were very pleased with the outcome and proposed to leave it to the 'open community' hosting the workshop! They had expressed a lot of envy and hostility to members of this community during the week and the 'devil's mask' was a container for this – but at the same time, it was something powerful and attractive to give to their rivals (see Plate 7a).

Group 2 had spent a lot of time deciding what to make before having the idea of a house on which they had written 'welcome' in many different languages. They felt that the group was like this house, full of different languages, different people, different problems. They wanted to make a comfortable and safe place for the group. It transpired that not all of them had felt welcomed in Italy (see Figure 22).

Group 3 had decided on 'love and hate'. N., who was a South American Indian, had made a model of a white man dominating a black man. He said that this was his symbol for 'hate'. The white man sat on a chair while the black man crouched on the ground (see Figure 23).

P., another black man, had made a model of an old man dressed in black. He said that for years his people had been dominated by white men.

The two black women in the group were in Group 2. They were also nuns and did not join the two men in the discussion about white domination. There was a general discussion in the group about which nationalities dominated others. I drew attention to my role as a white woman conductor, from a nation which had a history of dominating others. This comment was

Figure 23 Power struggles: black man and white man

accepted and my position acknowledged. P. said he had not really been aware of his 'blackness' till he saw N. making his figure and that led him to feel angry and wanting to make a statement about it. I mentioned again the question of my role as conductor, bearing in mind Yalom's point:

> The leader is [thus] seen unrealistically by members for many reasons: true transference or displacement of affect from some prior object is one source; conflicted attitudes toward authority – dependency, autonomy, rebellion and so on – which become personified in the therapist . . . still another source is the tendency to imbue the therapist with superhuman features so as to use him or her as a shield against existential anxiety. One further source lies in the members' explicit or intuitive appreciation of the great power of the group therapist. Your presence and your impartiality are . . . essential for group survival and stability. You cannot be deposed;

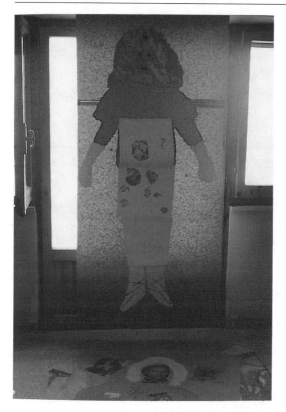

Figure 24 Image of pregnant woman with food under her skirt

you have at your disposal enormous power; you can expel members, add new members, mobilize group pressure against anyone you wish.

(1985: 210)

Yalom goes on to remind us that the sources of intense, irrational feelings towards the therapist are so powerful that transference will occur come what may. It is important to turn it to therapeutic account and to help members to recognise, understand and change their distorted attitudinal set towards the leader.

P.'s strong and clear statement about power and domination did, I think, contain much of the group's fantasies about my own power. This was particularly complex because of the composition of the group, containing as it did people with differing degrees of actual power (staff and residents from a 'closed community'). The ambivalence of the group towards me, expressed by Group 1's devil mask and the desire to be protected (the 'welcome' house) were all features of my role as conductor of this complex group.

In Group 4, people had chosen to work on their own theme. One woman said she had to stop because she was making a mother and child, but she could never have a child as a result of serious drug abuse. The realisation of this upset her, so she stopped making the figure and sat quietly in her group. Another woman, pregnant, made an elegant panther, and other group members made a child, a dog and a figure looking like Julius Caesar. I also felt the ambivalence towards 'Rome' as the place of training through the Julius Caesar figure. He is murdered in the forum, the place of democratic decision-making (group-as-forum where betrayals may take place and leaders be assassinated). I think my role as conductor was also included in this figure. There was another contrast between the fertile woman's panther and the sad image of the other woman whose fertility had been curtailed and between the child and dog (very friendly and nice) and the panther and Julius Caesar.

The discussion of all the material from the small groups took the whole of the next day. The sub-groups reflected aspects of the group-as-a-whole and particularly fantasies about the power of the conductor.

Following on from the symbols of power and domination contained in P.'s image of the white man dominating the black came the issue of sexuality. This discussion was reckoned by the group to be a difficult one for the following reasons:

- some members were priests and nuns and therefore other members perceived them as being 'shocked' by talk of sex, although they were not;
- some members feared HIV and AIDS as a result of sexual activity and drug abuse;
- several had always had profound anxiety about sex;
- one woman (staff member) was pregnant and was envied by others; there was a fantasy that she would have a 'virgin birth'. She was perceived as a mother figure (her portrait had been given plenty of good food by group members – interestingly enough, under her skirt) (see Figure 24).
- one member was both a Catholic and a homosexual and this was experienced as a sin.

The general feeling was that sex belonged in the 'evil' camp. At best it was unrewarding (with the notable exception of H. who was happily pregnant) and at worst it killed you (AIDS). These issues were able to be discussed as a result of the images now filling the room. Because sexuality was seen as the most difficult topic for the group, they left discussion of it until they were safe with each other and myself.

When it was time for that session to end, someone made the suggestion that the final session should be used to decide what to do with the artwork.

Case example 8

Splitting in the group
Forces of good and evil

This group is the same one mentioned in Case Example No. 7. The stage of the group I want to discuss follows the completion of the life-sized portraits and discussion of that process and focusses on the point where group members reflect on the symbolic selves around the room and decide what they wish to add or change to them.

One man, B., had made a portrait of himself instead of his partner (see Figure 25). He described it as absolutely right and he was satisfied at the negative image he had portrayed. Group members pointed out that he had ignored the task and his partner and he said he didn't care. He was very pleased with his painting. He sat with folded arms, looking both defiant and cheerful. Several members pointed out the devilish appearance of the painting and wondered why he had made it so evil-looking. It was covered with a huge spider's web which did look quite menacing.

The group were generally rather annoyed with his refusal to contemplate why he had ignored A. so that in fact he had two paintings of himself, one which A. had done and one he himself had done. (They had been used to working in groups where confrontation was the norm and where lack of consideration for others was discouraged.) B. had very elaborate tattoos on his arms and A. had put these on the painting (Plate 7b). B. was not happy about attention being drawn to them and wanted A. to remove them.

When it came to the time after the discussion when members could negotiate to work on any portrait, B. stood in front of his painting and said nobody was to touch it. Several people tried to persuade him to let them add something 'light' to the darkness of the painting but he refused angrily. One woman approached with a cut-out figure of a child which she wanted to place on the painting. He shouted at her to get out. She was the only one to persist in trying to interact with him and the painting and eventually he relented enough to draw a line across the bottom of the picture and allowed her to place cut-out figures there.

The group were interacting freely around the portraits. One man had negotiated with a pair (male and female) to place his painting between them, so they created a trio (see Plate 7c). Others negotiated to add, change, etc.

Figure 25 Devilish body image

The end of the session came and the room was left ready for the afternoon session.

When the group resumed, there was still some amending to be done but eventually people seemed satisfied that the 'symbolic group' was ready. We sat down to discuss the outcome. Much attention immediately focussed on B. for his attitude to others and his insistence on having all but a tiny piece of his painting untouched. He remained implacable and fought people off. Other people discussed how they had felt about the process and about changing images made by others. Then C. said that he felt very upset because nobody had been near his picture. He felt ignored by the group. C. was a priest, working in very difficult conditions in South America. He was a quiet man – the same man who had been involved in the spilling of water by S. He wondered why nobody had wanted to touch his painting. Members could not give him any response. They seemed to want to ignore even his request for feedback. There was more interest in pursuing B.'s refusal to have his painting touched.

I intervened to say that I felt that A. and C. represented two aspects of life

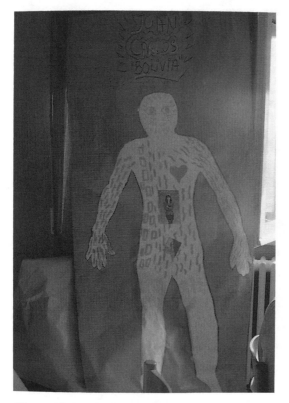

Figure 26 An unwilling icon

– and of the group – and that they had become polarised in the paintings. A. was clear that his painting was 'all evil' and he was not prepared to accept the positive feelings (in the form of additions and changes) that group members might have about him. A member intervened here to say that she had passed C.'s picture but hadn't dared touch it. It looked so 'perfect'. Others agreed and someone said the picture was like an icon. C. asked if it was because he was a priest that nobody dared touch him. He felt upset. He felt he had a problem in always looking after others throughout his life. Now he felt the group had made him into a saint and he did not want to be like that. He wanted to be a real person. He actually felt like a child. The group felt depressed and flat at this point, having split itself into two. As far as the group-as-a-whole were concerned, I felt the two images reflected the lack of integration in the composition of the group as well as a division into 'all good' and 'all evil', neither of which could be touched.

The group consisted of several sub-groups: staff and non-staff; residents of two different communities; Italian and non-Italian; ex-drug addicts and non-addicts; priests and nuns; men and women. There was also my position as conductor: good or evil, kind or punishing (similar to the dolphin–vulture images in Case Example No. 3). I put this to the group in connection with the group's paintings. The group were able to discuss their reactions to 'differences', especially between staff and residents and the polarities of 'good and evil'. During the discussion two people got up and added some marks to C.'s picture. One woman put a cut-out picture of a woman over his stomach, just under a heart, which someone else had drawn: she sensed he had some ambivalence about his chosen celibate role. Later he added a moustache, eyes and black spirals coming out of his head – taking a few 'devilish' elements from B.'s painting, making him feel less 'saintly'. Finally, a cut-out of a mountaineer appeared, placed underneath the woman's picture (see Figure 26).

Case example 9

Expressing anger symbolically

A group of seven women, all with eating disorders, had been meeting for over a year in a once-weekly group, for one and a half hours. There had been many problems in attendance and punctuality with excuses usually being that the woman had to attend to someone else (e.g. husband, children, mother) at the time of the group. The group was therefore somewhat fragmented and characterised by angry, envious feelings towards the therapist alternating with compliant, timid behaviour. The women found it difficult to confront each other verbally but did so through their artwork. A recurring complaint was of not being able to do what they really wanted, of being victims of circumstances outside their control. The word 'It' kept cropping up: 'It's not possible'; 'It won't happen'; 'I can't do It'; 'It's making me fat'; and so on.

The group noticed this word recurring over and over again in one session and decided to try to visualise exactly what 'It' was. The illustration (Figure 27) shows how 'It' looked to one group member, using torn up pieces of paper layered on top of each other. Another member drew an angry little devil on her shoulder. His claws are digging into her savagely (see Figure 28). Another drew a bomb exploding, and another a boulder rushing down a cliff. The feeling of these paintings was of tremendous energy being let loose, which the women felt was anger. They experienced anger as very dangerous, tended to dam it up and then to stuff themselves or alternatively starve themselves as a way of coping with it – or, indeed, with any strong and potentially creative feelings. The woman who drew the devil said she quite liked him after all but he should sit on her shoulder rather than claw her. Gradually, as the women got more familiar with the 'It' in each of them, they began to see that 'It' could be useful to them in providing them with more energy and vitality: which would be preferable to depression and stuffing or starving themselves (see also Levens, 1990 for an account of an interactive art therapy group with eating disordered clients).

Figure 27 'It' won't let me . . .

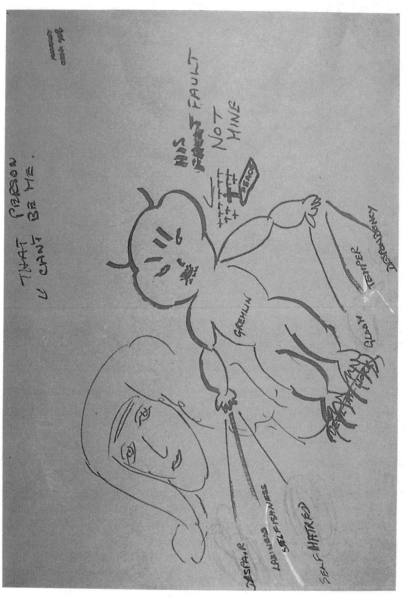

Figure 28 'It': a devilish figure

Example of a theme arising spontaneously

The art therapy department consisted of three rooms: one in which patients could use a wide variety of materials – paint, clay, mosaic and glass, and various other 3-D materials such as wood, cardboard boxes, 'junk'. One small room contained a kiln which was in constant use, and the other an easy chair and a couch, to which a patient could retire if feeling particularly emotionally drained or in need of privacy. The large room operated as a studio and patients could come and go as they wished during the time it was open. There were two part-time art therapists working on different days, and they were joined by a trainee who had expertise in pottery.

It was usual practice for the art therapists to make their own artwork. Nowadays, art therapists differ on this issue: some feel that if the therapist is engaged in their own image-making, they will not be 'available' for the group, others that the therapist can make statements visually about the group process as well as verbally. I have already explained that attempts to introduce more 'formal' groups into the art therapy department structure had not been popular but that more attention was being paid to interaction. The trainee, Jill, was persuaded by some of the male patients (who predominated in the centre and in the art department) to show them how to make moulds, out of which they could cast 'useful' objects. I had mixed feelings about this, fearing a 'production line' ethos developing in the art department which would be safer for the patients of course, as they would not risk being surprised or overwhelmed by unconscious material arising out of their image-making. It was a time of great insecurity in the centre as it had been threatened with closure once again and there were many disagreements among staff as to treatment policy. It was not surprising, then, that patients felt vulnerable and wanted to engage in a 'safe' activity. The group were divided into those who wanted to make moulds and do slip casting and those who wanted to continue with their own image-making.

I was absent from the centre for two weeks, but Jill had continued to use the art room with our colleague. When I returned I found the room full of plaster eggs, which had been cast from balloons – that is, a balloon is inflated and fine liquid plaster or slip is poured into it and allowed to set,

Figure 29 Birds and eggs

then the rubber is peeled off leaving a fragile egg shape. This was a technique which Jill had demonstrated, for fun, and which had caught on so that egg production had flourished and threatened to overwhelm the room. There was a competition to see who could produce the largest egg. There were, needless to say, many casualties. I wondered what to do about this proliferation, and sensed it had an important meaning. On asking about it, the patients pointed out that Easter was fast approaching and they were making them for that reason! I said that eggs usually contained embryo chicks and did they intend to make the chicks as well? Amid much mirth, all the group members joined in making chicks – having discovered a large bag of brightly coloured feathers in a cupboard. So the room became filled with eggs and chicks (see Figure 29).

Then one man, who had been at the centre for three years and who had severe relationship difficulties, especially with women, suggested making a 'large bird' and requested my help. The other members were intrigued as to how he would make it. He decided on papier mâché but first had to build a structure to support it. While the papier mâché was 'mulching' he found cardboard tubes and some wire and after discussion with myself, Jill and the other patients, built a slightly precarious base for the bird. There was the question of what to call it. Someone suggested Henry. As the papier mâché went on and the bird took shape, P. suggested it had better be called Henrietta as it was a female bird. There was then a group debate about whether or not it should be male or female. It became female. All group members took a turn in putting on the papier mâché and Jill and I also contributed. P. was asked to give her a 'sharp beak and beady eyes'. After the papier mâché dried, Henrietta got her feathers, beak and beady eyes (see Plate 8a).

Then there was the question of what to do with her. M., who had played a central role, with P., in the making, suggested suspending her from the ceiling so she could 'have a good fly around'. Someone else said 'She can keep an eye on you, then!' I had a strong sense that Henrietta was myself and/or my colleague. I had been absent for two weeks and the Easter break was approaching. The centre felt insecure. The making of Henrietta seemed to be a way in which the group were creating a 'symbolic mother' in the form of a bird who, although she had a sharp beak and beady eyes, would always be present in the room 'to keep an eye on things'. So she was fixed up on a piece of string and moved in the breeze created whenever the door was opened. The group then became concerned that she might be lonely up there, so K. suggested making a large spider to accompany her. P. said 'Henrietta will eat it!' They decided to make the spider after all and suspended it at a short distance from the bird, so that neither could get at the other. Someone asked 'Is it poisonous?' But the question was not answered. My colleague and I had the feeling that we were both represented in the spider and the bird – the spider seeming to be female also. We contained both dangerous and protective elements.

This is an example of how an apparently 'mechanical' activity, such as mould-making, may develop into an important interaction within the group, and one which can contain the anxiety of a group at a particular time. The making of the bird and the spider, although suggested by individuals, obviously resonated with other group members as all were involved at some level in the process. They remained, moving gently in the breeze, and were still there when I left the centre some two years later.

Case example 11

Boundary violation and scapegoating in a training group

This was a group of nine in an introductory art therapy programme lasting one week. It consisted of daily art therapy workshops run on an interactive model but with some initial setting of open-ended themes by myself. Some theoretical and practical media sessions were also included.

Many of the trainees had an art or art teaching background and were clear that the course was an introduction after which they might be able to consider taking further training in an Art Therapy programme. There were seven women and two men.

It is usual in this centre for the trainees and the conductors to have meals together and on the Sunday evening I encountered some of the participants in the dining room. I am usually friendly and willing to talk about art therapy in general but careful not to get involved in any more 'personal' discussion as it makes holding the boundaries of the course somewhat complicated. The participants sense this, as a rule, and normally we manage well over the week.

However, one participant wanted to engage me in intensive discussion. She did not speak English, however, and my understanding was fair but not good, so she asked another participant who spoke French to translate. She asked me for a critique of her artwork from the point of view of an art therapist. She had brought her work to the course for this purpose. I gently said that it was not part of my role to do this, and added that were I to see her artwork, my response would merely be a personal impression of the work, from one artist to another, so to speak. She was not happy with this and urged me to find time to see the work and offer her an 'analysis' of it. I repeated my previous comment and excused myself from the table. She was clearly put out by this and for a moment I wondered if I should have a look at the paintings but quickly concluded that I felt uncomfortable at the request because it implied she had not understood the purpose of the course (clearly advertised as an introductory course in art therapy with emphasis on group work) and wanted her own personal therapy. I made a mental note to stress in my introduction that the course was not therapy but that some personal learning may take place; that I should not be conducting the group as a therapist even though the group may wish to experience me like that from time to time.

On the first morning of the course I met the participants individually. One man was missing but I was told he would come later. I gave an introductory talk, with some basic theoretical material on art therapy and groups. I gave out the timetable, stressed the importance of time-keeping, no smoking, the limits of our working space and outlined the aims of the programme and my role in it. Dan then conducted a session on using art materials as they were not familiar with the nature of the materials on offer. I had found out during the brief interviews that some were studying architecture, one painted icons, one was a graphic designer, two were dancers and so on. 'Art' was interpreted in a broad sense.

For the first workshop, by way of an introduction to the process, I suggested that the participants think about themselves and the others in the group and without discussing it, select four members and make 'symbolic portraits' i.e. choose colours, shapes, images which suggested some aspects of those people. I said they would have the opportunity to talk about these pictures at the end of the week, if they wished to do so (to see if their perceptions had changed as a result of knowing each other better) and there would be a few minutes at the beginning of the next session to express feelings about the task itself. The aim was to encourage them to use the materials to make a spontaneous, based on initial impressions, non-verbal comment about others in the group.

They worked enthusiastically, and I noticed that they were experimenting with materials. When the end of the workshop approached, I advised them of the time and they finished on time.

The next morning the session began at 8.30 and a few people asked for some time to complete the previous day's work. I said perhaps this could be negotiated and they agreed among themselves to take half an hour including time for feeding back how they had felt about the task.

The next stage of the workshop was beginning the 'self-boxes' (see Chapter 3). While the the group were finishing their 'portraits' Gina, the interpreter, said quietly that M. had asked her to ask me to look at her paintings and make an analysis of them as she was going to have an exhibition and wanted to use my comments. She had felt that I didn't understand what she was asking the previous day so asked the interpreter to tell me in English. I was annoyed by this and let G. know that I could not deal with her request during the group. Later M. took G. aside and was obviously pressurising her to persuade me. This felt to me like M. not only ignoring what I had said to her the previous day but also breaking the boundaries of the conductor–interpreter relationship.

She was also again using an intermediary to ask for something: albeit there was a logical reason for the first request being translated as I did not speak Italian adequately (my problem) but on this occasion there seemed to be some desperation in her wanting my attention to her paintings. I wondered if I should bring it into the group but decided it was inappropriate at this point. I supposed the same issue would come up later, in the group. I felt M. was extremely anxious and was having difficulty being in the group. She was trying to deal with this by establishing a special relationship with myself. She also seemed to need the intermediary to communicate and so I thought that art therapy might be a useful form of *therapy* for her outside the course as the art object could serve as an intermediary. Gina must have said that I wasn't prepared to engage myself on this problem during the group. She was, fortunately, very sensitive to the boundaries herself. We carried on with the next part of the workshop, which was for each participant to select a box from a large and varied pile in a corner of the room.

Two women immediately had an altercation over the boxes as they both wanted the same one. One of them conceded to the other but took several boxes instead of one.

M. took a square box and stuffed it full of torn paper and a dead branch (driftwood which had been brought in as part of the 'junk box'), covered it up then wrapped it in tissue paper, brown sticky tape, sellotape so it was completely enclosed. Then she punched a hole in it and inserted a big tissue paper flower.

They all worked fast and energetically, using a lot of material. When everyone had clearly finished, S. asked if others would join him in talking about their boxes. One of the women, P. immediately started and a lively discussion followed in which each of the participants jostled to get a word in. They knew the end time but after R. had finished speaking I said it was time to end, giving the time of the next workshop session. M. immediately said she wanted to talk about hers. I said that the session had now ended. She said it was related to the previous box. I said the boxes would be there the next day and asked her to hold on till then. She was clearly furious with me.

The next session was a practical art materials workshop led by my colleague and in the evening there was a theoretical session during which time I showed some videos on art therapy.

The next morning we talked about the boxes again. M. brought in her box and banged it down in the centre of the group. It was tightly tied up and bound with only the bright blue flower sticking out. She said she felt the box was her and didn't want to speak about it but wanted others to comment. This provoked some anger from the group, especially S. and J. who asked 'What do you want of us?' W. was also angry. S. said he couldn't imagine opening the box and he didn't want to. This feeling seemed to be shared. The group members had seemed to draw back from the box. I was concerned that M. might be alienating herself and attracting the group anger. She seemed to see herself as the conductor, more experienced than the others, and I felt a strong challenge to me who had disappointed her and perhaps, she felt, rejected her by not providing her with an analysis of her paintings. Several group members pressured M. to share something about her box and she remained adamant that she only wanted others' comments. At this point it felt as if the group was 'stuck' with M.'s box and some participants said they were getting angry with her and not wanting to give their responses to her. I wondered if M. had only been able to introduce herself yesterday, at the end, in terms of R.'s openness and my reminding her of the end time had been experienced as 'cutting her off'. I tried to open the issue up by drawing attention to the different methods group members used to establish their role in the group and suggesting that perhaps M. was very anxious about getting into the group. At the same time I felt concerned about M. and her readiness to provoke the group's anger.

A. then said that my comment had modified what she had to say, which at first had been very judgemental. She felt able to make a less judgemental comment now because anxiety about being accepted belonged to her too and she thought to all the others.

M. couldn't take up this gesture to 'join' the group and dismissed A.'s comment angrily. The group tried to bring M. in to share in the anxiety about revealing themselves to each other. She would not budge from her previous position and suddenly tore and cut open her box. It was physically painful to watch and I felt a pain in my stomach and shortage of breath at that point. I looked round the group and saw other people holding their breath and looking shocked. A. commented that she thought M. could only open up in hostile conditions and it felt like rape or some kind of violence to the person. M. said, yes, she had been in that kind of situation in her family. M.'s box was spewing out torn up paper and a hunk of dead branch. People asked if the flower which had been sticking out was attached to anything or if it was superficial. There was a very tense atmosphere in the group, and it felt split between the dead branch and the flower. People seemed anxious to hear it was still growing. I pointed out this polarisation as a general point to the group and R. said 'That's enough of her box!' I was trying to hold onto the boundaries of an experiential group which was determined to become a therapy group. I made a few comments about the differences between the two, avoiding making a direct comment about M.'s drastic action but reminding members that it was up to each individual how much or how little – if anything at all – they said about their boxes.

After a short pause, shuffling and a sense of settling back, M. roughly brushed her box and its contents out of the centre and A. brought in hers. By contrast this was neat, made out of white polystyrene, lined with wall-paper. There was a little doll inside with pillows. She talked about her flight from 'sweetness' and started to cry. This was a total contrast to M.'s angry, hard presentation. The group were much involved in her story and there were positive, reinforcing comments made in response to her sadness and vulnerability as opposed to M.'s anger and mistrust. When A. had finished talking about her box, she gave M. the little doll with the comment: 'something tender to hold'. P. seemed very uncomfortable and kept restlessly silent. I sensed she found M.'s anger easier to deal with. E. brought her box in, half-open, half-closed with wings and flaps on top. She described punching holes in it with scissors which she had found liberating. There was a question 'Can some kinds of violence be liberating?' M. had opened her box with violence, but E. didn't want to open hers. I asked if the group had set a new a rule about having to open boxes. They said no, but they felt a pressure to do so and explored this for a while. I commented about the power of these previously mundane cardboard boxes to be symbols of so much, thus illustrating the point about the power of the object/image. I felt as if these comments were a bit banal in the face of so much emotional outpouring, but they did have the effect of maintaining the boundaries.

The group wrestled with the decision whether to carry on talking about the boxes or to stop and move on. There was concern that three people hadn't spoken about theirs. They remained silent. I said that perhaps it was permissible for this to happen. After a silence I suggested some of the themes which the group had been dealing with as a result of the boxes: polarisation; being an individual in a group; trusting or not; being open or not; being angry and hard – or being hurt and vulnerable. Also the important question which was raised – could violence ever be positive? Someone said feelings of anger and vulnerability often went together and it was confusing to experience these strong emotions together. The discussion moved on to relationships and how you could love someone but be angry and vulnerable with them.

A. and S. said they wanted me to make comments – to clear up the confusion. S. said perhaps the end of the week would provide the revelation! There was laughter after which I pointed out where and why I had intervened and said that I felt they had plenty of resources too. The group ended with people going off quietly and thoughtfully.

In the next workshop we took the theme of relationships and maintaining individuality in a group a bit further. I asked them to work in three groups of three and proposed that they could either group together (choose each other) or pick names out of a hat. Everyone wanted to do the latter. So Gina pulled the names out in threes. The task was to find some way of building an environment for their boxes which would involve negotiation and perhaps some compromise. Interestingly, one of the groups consisted of M., P. and E. who had had the most angry exchanges during the previous workshop. They were not pleased at working together and went off sulkily. All the groups spent quite a bit of time in discussion, and it was clear that M., P. and E. were having difficulty in working. The other two groups appeared to have made decisions. One group checked with everyone that it was permissible to go onto the balcony and the other to the back of the room

Figure 30 Making an environment

among the potted plants. M.'s group eventually started to construct an environment in the middle of the room and they worked on it in a polite but cool manner. The other groups were laughing a lot and seemed engrossed in the task. I wondered about the 'luck of the draw' as far as M., P. and E. were concerned. The session ended and everyone went off. I noticed that M., P. and E. avoided each other after the group ended.

Early the next morning the elements made the decision 'where to start' for the group. There was a huge storm brewing: high wind, very dark sky, menacing atmosphere. The group on the balcony anxiously went to look at their environment. They said they had trusted that it would remain intact overnight but if the elements had affected the construction that was fine because it was OK for it to be changed by the elements.

They had made a path going from the door of the studio towards the sea and put a large sheet of paper, like a flag, on the railing of the balcony. The wind had torn some of it but most was still intact. They had brought the boxes inside overnight, just in case. They said their environment felt hopeful – exposed to sun and wind but rescued just before the storm. They laughed and said 'This is the calm before the storm!' I had a sense of foreboding. They said they had arrived at an environment which took care of everyone's wishes and were satisfied with it (see Figures 30 and 31).

When we went inside, I had a shock as I felt something had changed from

Figure 31 Making an environment

the previous day. In fact, although I was sure, I persuaded myself my memory was defective. It was not, however.

There were big problems about M., P. and E.'s group and it turned out that M. had gone back to the studio late in the afternoon/evening (we were away from the centre at that time) and had totally changed the group's environment. She had made it her own by painting a huge blue area, representing water, on which was an island, adding the piece of dead branch and arranging it so it crushed a small doll (which A. had given her from her box). M. sat on a chair, away from P. and E. who were standing to one side looking upset and angry. She said for her the therapy finished yesterday evening. She then proceeded to go through the events of the week in a very detailed way, in an aggressive tone – a monologue. I intervened to point out that she was delivering a lecture and was it relevant to the work done together? I wondered, further, why M. had taken on, and been allowed by her group, to take on the position of spokeswoman and what had happened to her two colleagues? I also pointed out that a boundary had been broken and that a space was no longer safe if boundaries were violated in such a manner. I repeated the boundaries of time and space which I'd stated clearly at the beginning. I had not actually *said* that nobody should enter the studio in between sessions. It was kept locked but M. had got the key from the centre staff! She denied that there was a problem and said she didn't know it was not 'allowed' to use the studio outside course sessions. E. was furious with M. for 'wiping out' their communal work and for not even acknowledging the fact. A. was extremely upset that the doll she had given M. the previous day had been treated in such a way. She felt it personally.

There was an interesting difference between the changes in the environment brought about by the wind in the first group – who had made the decision to leave it exposed and able to change – and those made deliberately but without negotiation by M. The whole group turned on M. who sat defiant on her chair, hitting out at everyone. I felt myself becoming angry with her too so thought it was time to draw attention to the group dynamic of polarisation again. I was conscious that M. did not have a sense of her own boundaries and feared that she had deeply distressing early material which was coming to the surface in this training group, which was not the right arena to deal with it. Had it been a therapy group, the personal material would no doubt have been brought in and worked through by M. and the group over a period of time. This was a course with experiential groups, lasting one week, after which the group would cease to exist. It was hard to keep maintaining didactic boundaries. I had felt M. in particular, was trying to lead the group into a therapy group again, having failed to establish a one-to-one relationship with me earlier on. I felt decidedly anxious about containing her in the group as her personal boundaries seemed very disturbed and I sensed she was holding on to highly distressing personal material, almost wanting the group to 'guess it'.

I put forward the notion of 'taking on roles' in a group and asked P. and E. to reflect on their own role as well as M.'s. I suggested M. was investing a lot of energy in keeping separate from the rest of the group, even though she was a member of it. I tried to find M. some companions, i.e. to see if there were other participants who would have liked to change their environment after the workshop. She was now in serious danger of becoming scapegoated as several people said they didn't want to listen to her any more. I felt it was important to make whole-group interventions, which would prevent M. from becoming isolated and charged with the rage of the whole group. Nobody said they wanted to change the environment – indeed several people were adamant that they had spent a lot of time in negotiating theirs and were satisfied with the result. I was conscious of M.'s two colleagues' fury (and with some justification of course as their joint efforts had been wiped out by M.) to one side of me. It was clear that they were disappointed by her implacable denial of their position and lack of understanding about their hurt and anger at their joint work being erased. There was nothing more to be done at that point; the group had to 'live with' the wretched feelings, and after my brief 'lecture' on roles it felt appropriate, and indeed a relief, to move on to the final group's work.

This group was a total contrast in its lack of obvious conflict and indeed some members suggested that all the 'bad feeling' was in the neighbouring environment. This led to a discussion of war and projecting all the negative onto another country or people or neighbour or spouse, etc. R., S. and T. said they had become conscious of the anger in the nearby group and wanted to withdraw to a quiet place and make an 'idyllic' landscape with flowers, trees, sea and sun. There was, however, a large, spiky, phallic cactus in the centre of the scene which members pointed out as the sexual element intervening (like the serpent in the Garden of Paradise) (see Plate 8b).

A general discussion of the three groups followed in which the main issue was boundary violation, clearly acted out by M. but also discussed in terms of war and trespass on others' space. The storm had broken and the outside environment was being torn down by the wind and rain – elements outside ourselves – the cactus reminding people of the power of sexuality and that it could be abusive (as in rape or inappropriate sexual relations) or creative. The session ended with these reflections.

The teaching points were numerous from these workshops but the group had totally absorbed the importance of maintaining the boundaries as a result of the 'acting out' and being able to discuss it symbolically through their environments and actually by reference to how they themselves felt when it happened. They were able to link it to the 'outside' i.e. to social conflict, sexual abuse, violation of others' physical and emotional space, and finally to war among nations. They had also learned about scapegoating and feeling powerless to change a situation.

Working through a crisis

The group was in the second phase of a three-part intensive block training in Bulgaria, based on three participating centres. The week had been very fraught for the following reasons.

(a) The course was taking place in a hospital far from the capital. Relations between the medical centres were somewhat strained.
(b) There had been problems with materials and no clay could be found in the city; it was not certain that we could have a video-playback machine.
(c) The weather was unusually cold (snowing) for that time of year and the heating was inadequate or non-existent in places.
(d) The conductors and course co-ordinators had a very bad journey from the capital, as all direct flights had been cancelled and they were obliged to take a plane to the nearest city and find alternative means of transport to the hospital. Thus they arrived late, tired and very cold on the night before the course started.
(e) The conductors and co-ordinators were staying in the hospital whereas the participants were staying in hotels in the city, some several kilometres away with infrequent transport.
(f) The participants had not been advised of the timetable, in particular the starting time of the course!

The course started late on the Monday morning due to accommodation and transport problems and on Tuesday, none of the Sofia participants arrived! Another participant rushed in late to say that the Sofia group had had to leave their hotel because the management wanted to give their rooms to Western tourists with hard currency. (This, unfortunately, was not an unusual situation as the economy was in trouble and the country desperately needed convertible currency.)

The Sofia group were now wandering around the town looking for accommodation which apparently was very scarce. There was anger, confusion and chaos – I was angry about the appalling disruption to precious training time and with the 'system' for permitting such callous treatment. I felt my only course of action was to speak to the hospital chief

Figure 32 Going away to the West

as he might have been able to intervene. In fact, by a joint effort we managed to get the Sofia group restored to their hotel but of course we lost most of that day's coursework.

Being an interactive course, however, the situation gave rise to material which could be used in the groups.

On the following morning, everyone arrived still angry and depressed at their overall situation: this included the participants who lived in the town or had been staying elsewhere. There was some hostility between these different groups of participants. We sat in silence for a while until one participant suggested making a painting about the group's experience of this incident at the hotel. Everyone fell on the suggestion and the group worked

Figure 33 Detail of 'Going away to the West' showing gun, passport, cheque book and dictionary

feverishly for the rest of the workshop. The resulting painting was very violent and the Greek visitors had been thoroughly destroyed. The event had aroused memories of old conflicts with Greeks. There was rage that the Greeks could take precedence, just because they had hard currency. I felt very uncomfortable during this painting time because I knew that the group were also furious with me for having privileges, although they also knew that I was opposed to the 'second class' status these people felt, and experienced, in their own country. There were similarities in this situation to the 'Julius Caesar' issue in Case Example No. 7.

In the next session people said they felt exhausted but very good as a lot of anger had been discharged into the painting. They also felt guilty because they had taken their anger out on the Greeks who were not actually responsible personally. I raised the issue of Westerners coming in and taking over and wondered if they had some feelings about myself, as the conductor. There was debate as to whether or not I was really a Westerner. Were all Westerners superior and exploitative? The conclusion was that I was only partly a Westerner! On the other hand, they brought hard currency and some good things (like art therapy . . .). This feeling was reflected later in the week. Much time was spent on the group's inability to resist being thrown out of the hotel because of fear of reprisal (not a fantasy, I should say). However, as a group of psychiatrists in a high level project, they could have made an attempt to explain their situation. Very useful discussion took place about power relations and taking out anger on people who were not responsible for the situation.

On the following day, they decided to paint as a group and had much fun dribbling paint and using finger-paint, etc. It seemed as if the group had regressed to early childhood and were enjoying themselves. Yet there was a large spider's web, which grew and somewhat dominated the picture, slightly menacing.

On the final day, the group decided to make an image of a woman (see Figure 32) who was going to travel to the West. It was decided to send her to New York. They discussed what she should look like and what she should take with her. She was given a smart dress and boots, an English–Bulgarian dictionary, a headband with the colours of the Bulgarian flag, passport, cheque book, cash, food and a gun (see Figure 33).

The person who made the gun said there were a lot of criminals in New York and she needed to protect herself. I felt that this woman was actually me as I was going away – to the West – but I would go back because I still had my Bulgarian passport. There was laughter and tears – I felt moved and also close to tears, and very much part of the group. The woman was a bridge between East and West and the image was so loaded with meanings on so many levels – personal and political. I felt part of me was really in the image and compelling me to go away yet go back – even though the whole week had been difficult and 'heavy' with impending crises. I was actually relieved to see she had a return ticket. It was a powerful example of the image taking one over, or, technically, of projective identification.

In writing up this piece now, I still feel very moved and aware of the massive changes that have happened since that workshop. The fantasies about 'the West' as a place where all was good (except for the criminals) and the 'East' so bad were very strong. Of course, the fantasies were fed by events such as the one described above, by effective propaganda from Western media and by a deteriorating economic situation.

As a conductor, with my own personal history of involvement with 'the East' I could not feel myself totally identified with 'the West'. Yet undeniably I could move in and out freely whereas the group members could not. This was reality, not fantasy on their behalf. So I could be both of 'the East' and 'the West'. I believe these elements were magnificently portrayed in the final painting of that course.

Ending the group
What to do with the images and objects

Of course, each group finds its own way to resolve this problem. Unlike in a verbal group, when participants take themselves out of the room and out of the process, the interactive art therapy group has usually produced a large number of objects – symbolic selves, in fact.

Deciding what to do with these objects is an important part of the process, I believe. The objects belong to the group: they have reflected its process as well as the process of each individual. Who do they really belong to?

If they are simply left behind, the onus is on the conductor to dispose of them. This is rather difficult as they may still contain powerful symbolic content – apart from the practical difficulties of disposing of many large constructions and paintings.

One can never know what objects will be made and how they will occupy space. The ending has to include the objects. Some will have lost their symbolic content during the group – a picture that was so frightening or difficult to deal with on the first day may be seen in a different perspective at the end.

Groups can be very creative about resolving this problem. One student group, after a year's experiential workshops, decided to burn all the paintings in an end-of-year ceremony. Building the bonfire (containing it safely was important) and placing the work on it was like a 'happening'. I believe that some people saved a few pieces which they wanted to work on further themselves, but the group celebrated its end by the ritual fire.

A less dramatic way was as follows. All the paintings were removed from the wall by their original painter; they were rolled up. Boxes were assembled in a corner with space enough in between each for them to be picked up by their maker. Clay objects were placed on a board. Constructions made by the group were de-constructed carefully and the bits laid to one side. Individuals decided what to keep and what to throw away. Joint works had to be argued over but usually got thrown away. Some pieces were offered to the host community.

After the selection was made and unwanted pieces discarded, the room

Figure 34 The end of a week-long workshop

Figure 35 Clearing up

was thoroughly cleaned by all concerned. Even the floor washing became a ritual in itself, and appeared as a piece of choreography (see Figures 34 and 35). When the room was entirely stripped of all remnants of the group, all left together.

This is, to my mind, an essential aspect of an interactive art therapy group. The interactions between members at this stage are often very moving and lead people gradually out of one stage and into another (the outside world). This is a very important transitional stage and when structuring a course – or working with a time-limited group, I always make sure there is adequate time for this process. I try to end a training group by reflecting back myself on some of the processes that have gone on, and encourage the group to do the same. It is useful at this point to make some connections with the theoretical underpinning of the group.

When ending a patient group, it is often the case that the patients themselves want to look back and review how much they have changed over the period of the group. Usually they want to take their individual pieces of artwork away. The group may offer group paintings to the conductor, or decide other ways of taking or leaving composite works. It can happen that a member doesn't turn up for the last session – separation still being far too powerful to face in reality, in which case the group has to deal with this issue and the conductor and the group with their remaining artwork. In practical terms, I would write to the member asking if they want individual pieces of work, but in dynamic terms, there is little that can be done at that stage.

Sorting and reflecting on the work, tidying and cleaning the room, breaks the spell of the powerful group process and enables each member to claim back and take responsibility for their contribution to the work and to the changes in their lives.

Appendix
Where to find information about group therapy and art therapy

There are numerous journals giving information about training and events in psychotherapy and art therapy. The following are a few starting points for more specialised information.

GENERAL INFORMATION

British Association of Art Therapists, 11A Richmond Road, Brighton BN23RL. BAAT is the professional association of art therapists and provides a useful information brochure, list of publications, bibliography and occasional pamphlets on aspects of the profession. Write, enclosing an sae for information.

The Group Analytic Society, 1 Daleham Gardens, London NW3 5BY. The Society has several categories of membership, including full membership for qualified and practising group analysts. It provides a full programme of lectures and events, many open to the public.

British Association for Counselling, 37A Sheep Street, Rugby CV21 3BX. The association is open to professionals practising counselling, including group therapy. It publishes a useful journal with much information about training courses, study weekends, etc., in counselling and psychotherapy.

TRAINING IN ART THERAPY

Art Psychotherapy Unit, Goldsmiths' College, University of London, 23 St James, New Cross, London SE14 6AD.

Postgraduate Arts Therapies Programme, Hertfordshire College of Art and Design, 7 Hatfield Road, St Albans, Herts.

Centre for Art and Psychotherapy Studies, Floor O, Department of Psychiatry, Royal Hallamshire Hospital, Glossop Road, Sheffield Sl0 2JF.

All the above offer courses ranging from Foundation Studies, Diploma (2 years full time) to Masters and MPhil/PhD programmes. The Diploma courses are recognised by the BAAT, the Department of Health and the National Joint Council as qualifying graduates to practise art therapy. These centres also run short courses.

TRAINING IN GROUP PSYCHOTHERAPY

Art Psychotherapy Unit, Goldsmiths' College, University of London, 23 St James, New Cross, London SE14 6AD. Three-year part-time postgraduate or post-experience Diploma in Group Psychotherapy. Also runs foundation studies and short courses in specialised areas, for example, Large Group Dynamics. The Unit has developed a research programme to investigate multi-cultural issues in psychotherapy training.

Institute of Group Analysis, 1 Daleham Gardens, London NW3 5BY. Runs introductory and qualifying programme in Group Analytic Psychotherapy and with the Group Analytic Society above, short courses and weekend workshops for professional staff. IGA is developing a regional training network and assists in setting up training abroad.

Bibliography

Agazarian, Y. and Peters, R. (1989) *The Visible and Invisible Group: Two Perspectives on Group Psychotherapy and Group Process*, Tavistock/Routledge, London. (First published 1981, Routledge & Kegan Paul.)

Astrachan, B. (1970) 'Towards a social systems model of therapy groups', *Social Psychiatry*, 5, 110–19.

Attenborough, Sir Richard (1985) *Arts and Disabled People. Report of a Committee of Inquiry*, Carnegie UK Trust, Bedford Square Press, London.

Aveline, M. and Dryden, W. (1988) *Group Therapy in Britain*, Open University Press, Milton Keynes.

Aveline, M. and Dryden, W. (1988) 'A comparative review of small group therapies', in M. Aveline and W. Dryden (eds), *Group Therapy in Britain*, Open University Press, Milton Keynes.

Bandura, A. (1977) *Social Learning Theory*, Prentice Hall, Englewood Cliffs, NJ.

Barron, F. (1968) *Creativity and Personal Freedom*, D. Van Nostrand & Co., Princetown.

Bierer, J. (ed.) (1948) *Therapeutic Social Clubs*, H.K. Lewis, London.

Bion, W.R. (1961) *Experiences in Groups and Other Papers*, Tavistock, London.

Bion, W.R. (1962) *Learning from Experience*, Heinemann, London.

Bion, W.R. and Rickman, J. (1943) 'Intra-group tensions in therapy: their study as the task of the group', *Lancet* ii, 678–81.

Bloch, S. (1979) 'Assessment of patients for psychotherapy', *British Journal of Psychiatry*, 135, 193–208.

Bloch, S. (1982) *What is Psychotherapy?* Oxford University Press, Oxford.

Bloch, S. and Crouch, E. (1985) *Therapeutic Factors in Group Psychotherapy*, Oxford University Press, Oxford.

Blos, P. (1962) *On Adolescence*, Free Press, New York.

Bridger, H. (1946) 'The Northfield Experiment', *Bulletin of the Menninger Clinic* 10 (3), 71–76.

Case, C. and Dalley, T. (eds) (1990) *Working with Children in Art Therapy*, Routledge, London.

Champernowne, I. (1969) 'Art therapy as an adjunct to psychotherapy', *Inscape Journal of Art Therapy*, 1.

Cohn, R. R. (1969) 'Psychoanalytic or experiential group psychotherapy: a false dichotomy', *Psychoanalytic Review* 50, 110–19.

Corsini, R. and Rosenberg, B. (1955) 'Mechanisms of group psychotherapy process and dynamics', *Journal of Abnormal and Social Psychology* 51, 406–11.

Dalley, T. (ed.) (1984) *Art as Therapy*, Tavistock/Routledge, London.

Drucker, K. 1990 'Swimming upstream: art therapy with the psychogeriatric population in one health district', in M. Liebmann (ed.) *Art Therapy in Practice*, Jessica Kingsley, London.

Durkin, H.E. (1974) 'Current problems of group psychotherapy in historical context', in L.R. Wolberg, M.L. Aronson and A.R. Wolberg (eds) *Group Therapy: 1974, An Overview*, Stratton Intercontinental Medical Book Corp, New York.

Durkin, H.E. (1982) 'Change in group psychotherapy practice: a systems perspective', *International Journal for Group Psychotherapy* 32, 431–9.

Ezriel, H. (1950) 'A psychoanalytic approach to group treatment', *British Journal of Medical Psychology* 23, 57–74.

Fielden, T. (1990) 'Art therapy as part of the world of dyslexic children', in M. Liebmann (ed.) *Art Therapy in Practice*, Jessica Kingsley, London. pp. 104–13.

Foulkes, S.H. (1948) *Introduction to Group Analytic Psychotherapy*, Maresfield Reprints, London.

Foulkes, S.H. (1975) *Group Analytic Psychotherapy. Method and Principles*, Gordon & Breach, London.

Foulkes, S.H. (1983) 'A basic law of group dynamics', in *Introduction to Group Analytic Psychotherapy*, Maresfield Reprints, London. pp. 29–30.

Foulkes, S.H. and Anthony, E.J. (1965) *Group Psychotherapy: The Psychoanalytic Approach* (2nd edn), Penguin, Harmondsworth.

Fried, E. (1975) 'Building psychic structures as a prerequisite for change', *International Journal for Group Psychotherapy* 25, 251–75.

Fromm, E. (1973) 'Freud's concept of man and its social determinants', in E.G. Witenberg (ed.) *Interpersonal Explorations in Psychoanalysis. New Directions in Theory and Practice*, Basic Books, New York. (Originally in E. Fromm (1970) *The Crisis of Psychoanalysis*, Holt Rinehart & Winston Inc., New York.)

Greenwood, H. and Layton, G. (1987) 'An out-patient art therapy group', *Inscape Journal of Art Therapy*, Summer, pp. 12–19.

Hill, A. (1945) *Art versus Illness*, London, Allen & Unwin.

Holmes, P. (1991) 'Classical psychodrama: an overview', in P. Holmes and M. Karp, *Psychodrama: Inspiration and Technique*, Routledge, London. pp. 7–13.

Kernberg, O.F. (1975) 'A systems approach to priority setting of interventions in groups', *International Journal of Group Psychotherapy* 25, 251–75.

Levens, M. (1990) 'Borderline aspects in eating disorders', *Group Analysis* 33 (3), 277–84.

Lewin, K. (1948) *Resolving Social Conflicts*, Harper & Row, New York.

Lewin, K. (1951) *Frontiers in Group Dynamics*, Harper & Row, New York.

Liebmann, M.F. (1979) 'A study of structured art therapy groups', Unpublished MA thesis, Birmingham Polytechnic, UK.

Liebmann, M.F. (1982) *Art Games and Structures for Groups*, Bristol Art Therapy Group, Bristol.

Liebmann, M.F. (1986) *Art Therapy for Groups: A Handbook of Themes, Games and Exercises*, Croom Helm, London. (Reprinted by Routledge, 1989.)

Liebmann, M.F. (1990) *Art Therapy in Practice*, Jessica Kingsley, London.

Linesch, D. Greenspoon (1988) *Adolescent Art Therapy*, Brunner-Mazel, New York.

Littlewood, R. and Lipsedge, M. (1982) *Aliens and Alienists: Ethnic Minorities and Psychiatry*, Penguin, London.

Maclagan, D. (1985) 'Art therapy in a therapeutic community', *Inscape Journal of Art Therapy*, late edition, London, pp. 7–8.

McNeilly, G. (1983) 'Directive and non-directive approaches in art therapy', *The Arts in Psychotherapy* 10 (4), 211–219. (Reprinted in *Inscape*, December 1984.)

McNeilly, G. (1987) 'Further contributions to group analytic art therapy', *Inscape Journal of Art Therapy*, Summer, pp. 8–11.

McNeilly, G. (1990) 'Group analysis and art therapy: a personal perspective', Special Section edited by D. Waller in *Group Analysis and the Arts Therapies, in Group Analysis* 23 (3), 215–24.

Main, T.F. (1946) 'The Northfield Experiment', *Bulletin of the Menninger Clinic* 10 (3), 71–6.

Matthews, J. (1989) 'How young children give meaning to drawing', in A. Gilroy and T. Dalley (eds) *Pictures at an Exhibition*, Tavistock/Routledge, London. pp. 127–42.

Messer, S.B. (1986) 'Eclecticism in psychotherapy. Underlying assumptions, problems and trade-offs', in J.C. Norcross (ed.) *Handbook of Eclectic Psychotherapy*, Brunner-Mazel, New York, pp. 379–97.

Milner, M. (1950) *On Not Being Able to Paint*, Heinemann, London.

Milner, M. (1969) *The Hands of the Living God*, Hogarth Press, London.

Molloy, T. (1984) 'Art therapy and psychiatric rehabilitation: harmonious partnership or philosophical collision?' *Inscape Journal of Art Therapy*, August, pp. 2–10.

Nowell Hall, P. (1987) 'Art therapy: a way of healing the split', in T. Dalley, C. Case, D. Halliday, J. Schaverien, P. Nowell Hall, F. Weir and D. Waller (eds) *Images of Art Therapy*, Routledge, London. pp. 157–86.

Ratigan, B. and Aveline, M. (1988) 'Interpersonal group therapy', in M. Aveline and W. Dryden *Group Therapy in Britain*, Open University Press, Milton Keynes. pp. 43–64.

Roberts, J. (1985) 'Resonance in art groups', *Group Analysis*, December. pp. 211–20. *Inscape Journal of Art Therapy*, Summer, pp. 17–20. (First printed in *Group Analysis*, December 1984, 211–20.)

Rogers, C. (1957) 'The necessity, and sufficient conditions of therapeutic change', *Journal of Consulting Psychology* 22, 95–103.

Ruitenbeek, H.M. (1970) *The New Group Therapies*, Discus Books, Avon, New York.

Schafer, R. (1976) *A New Language for Psychoanalysis*, Yale University Press, London.

Schafer, R. (1983) *The Analytic Attitude*, Hogarth Press, London.

Skaife, S. (1990) 'Self-determination in group analytic art therapy', *Group Analysis* 23 (3), 237–44.

Skynner, A.R. (1976) *One Flesh, Separate Persons*, Constable, London.

Slavson, S.R. (1950) *Analytic Group Psychotherapy*, Columbia University Press, New York.

Stack Sullivan, H. (1953) *The Interpersonal Theory of Psychiatry*, W.W. Norton Inc., New York.

Strand, S. (1990) 'Counteracting isolation: group art therapy for people with learning difficulties', *Group Analysis* 23 (3), 255–63.

Sutherland, J.D. (1985) 'Bion revisited: group dynamics and group psychotherapy', in M. Pines (ed.) *Bion and Group Psychotherapy*, Routledge, London. pp. 47–86.

Thompson, S. and Khan, J. (1988) *The Group Process and Family Therapy*, Pergamon Press, Oxford.

Thornton, R. (1985) 'Review of Gerry McNeilly's article: Directive and non-directive approaches in art therapy', *Inscape Journal of Art Therapy*, Summer, pp. 23–4.

Tipple, R. (1992) 'Art therapy with people with learning difficulties', in D. Waller and A. Gilroy (eds) *Art Therapy in Britain*, Open University Press, Milton Keynes.

Wadeson, H. (1980) *Art Psychotherapy*, John Wiley, New York.

Wadeson, H. (1987) *The Dynamics of Art Psychotherapy*, John Wiley, New York.

Waller, D. (1983/84) 'Art therapy in Bulgaria. Parts I and II', *Inscape Journal of Art Therapy*, April and October, pp. 12–15, 15–17.

Waller, D. (1990) 'Art therapy in Bulgaria. Part III', *Inscape Journal of Art Therapy*, Summer, pp. 26–32.

Waller, D. (1991) *Becoming a Profession: The History of Art Therapy in Britain, 1940–1982*, Routledge, London.

Winnicott, D.W. (1951) 'Transitional objects and transitional phenomena', in *Collected Papers: Through Paediatrics to Psychoanalysis*, Tavistock, London.

Winnicott, D.W. (1971) *Therapeutic Consultations in Child Psychiatry*, Hogarth Press, London.

Wood, C. (1992) 'Art therapy with chronically mentally ill patients', in D. Waller and A. Gilroy (eds) *Art Therapy in Britain*, Open University Press, Milton Keynes.

Yalom, I. (1985) *The Theory and Practice of Group Psychotherapy* (1st edn 1975), Basic Books, New York.

Yalom, I. (1983) *In-patient Group Psychotherapy*, Basic Books, New York.

Name index

Agazarian, Yvonne 3, 30–2, 104
Anthony, E.J. 15, 81
Astrachan, B. 3, 29–30
Aveline, M. 3, 5, 22–3, 42–4, 49

Bandura, A. 44
Bierer, Joshua 5, 7
Bion, Wilfred R. 5, 16–17, 33
Bloch, S. 3, 22, 25–7, 28, 30, 32
Blos, P. 83
Blume, Peter 55
Bridger, Harold 5

Caro, Anthony 55
Case, C. 82
Champernowne, Dr Irene 8, 45
Christo 55
Cizek, Franz 46
Cohn, R.R. 28–9
Conner, Bruce 55
Corsini, R. 25
Crouch, E. 3, 22, 25–7, 28, 30, 32

Dalley, T. 10, 11, 82
Drucker, K. 74–5
Dryden, W. 5, 42–3, 49
Dubuffet, Jean 55
Dudley, Jane 9
Durkin, H.E. 28, 30

Ezriel, Henry 5, 24

Fielden, Trish 82
Foulkes, S.H. 3, 5, 14–15, 81
Freud, Sigmund 6, 22, 31
Fried, E. 30
Fromm, Erich 25
Frye, Northrop 43

Gilroy, Andrea 9
Greenwood, Helen, 16–17

Hill, Adrian 7, 8
Holmes, P. 40
Horney, Karen 25

Jung, Carl 9

Kernberg, O.F. 30
Khan, J. 27, 44–5
Kienholz, Edward 55

Layton, Geoff 16–17
Levens, M. 19, 130
Lewin, Kurt 5–6, 31
Liebmann, Marion F. 10–14, 82
Linesch, D. Greenspoon 82–4
Lipsedge, M. 6
Littlewood, R. 6
Lumley, Dan 54

Maclagan, David 17–18, 37, 52–3
McNeilly, Gerry 3, 9, 10, 11–13, 14–16,
    19, 33, 46–7
Main, Tom 5
Matthews, J. 37
Messer, S.B. 43
Milner, M. 8
Molloy, T. 75–7

Nevelson, Louise 55
Nowell Hall, Patricia 45–6, 47–8

Peters, R. 3, 30–2

Ratigan, B. 3, 22–3, 43–4
Richardson, Marion 46
Rickman, J. 5
Roberts, J. 15
Rogers, Carl 45–6
Rosenberg, B. 25
Ruitenbeek, H.M. 6, 29

Subject index